HEALTHY AND EASY CROCK POT COOKBOOK:

Tasty Slow Cooker / Crock Pot Recipes for Beginners

By
Lisa Clark

TABLE OF CONTENTS

INTRODUCTION

Ever feel like there aren't enough hours in the day? Us too. That's where the crock pot comes in. It would be unfair to call it t a kitchen gadget; it's like having a cooking fairy godparent, turning everyday ingredients into mouthwatering dishes for you.

Life is crazy busy, right? But what if we told you there's a way to make amazing meals without stressing out? It's not fancy; it's just a pot that works its magic while you go about your day. And the best part? The food tastes like you spent all day cooking.

Now, let's talk about what's coming up. This isn't your regular cookbook. It's more like a guide to making life in the kitchen a breeze. Whether you're a kitchen pro or a total newbie, the crock pot is here to make your cooking life easy and tasty. No need to be a chef; the crock pot does the hard work, and you get all the credit.

Getting Started with Your Crock Pot

If you're staring at this magical kitchen gadget and wondering where to begin, don't worry – we've got your back. We'll guide you through the basics and make your crock pot cooking experience a delicious success.

Unbox and Get Familiar

First things first, take your crock pot out of the box. It might look like a high-tech device, but don't be intimidated – it's your new kitchen buddy. Most crock pots have two parts: a pot and a base. The pot is where the magic happens, and the base is what heats it. Simple, right?

Prep Like a Pro

Before you start throwing ingredients into the pot, a little prep work goes a long way. Chop your veggies, trim your meat, and gather your spices. It's like a kitchen party before the crock pot takes over the dance floor. Bonus tip: For easy cleanup, consider using cooking spray or liners in the pot.

Layering Goodness

Here's a secret: layering is key. Start with the heartiest ingredients at the bottom – think potatoes, carrots, or chunks of meat. Then, pile on the softer stuff like beans or peas. This way, everything cooks evenly, and you get a symphony of flavors in every bite.

Add the Liquid Love

No crock pot dish is complete without some liquid love. Whether it's broth, sauce, or just plain water, this is what keeps everything moist and oh-so-tender. The rule of thumb? Enough to cover the ingredients but not drown them. You're aiming for a cozy simmer, not a swimming pool.

Spice It Up

Now comes the fun part – the spices! Don't be shy; this is where you make the dish yours. Salt, pepper, garlic powder, paprika – go wild. Experiment with flavors until you find your perfect combo. And don't forget herbs; they're like little flavor fairies sprinkling magic over your meal.

Set It and Forget It

Once everything is in the pot and seasoned to perfection, it's time to let the crock pot work its magic. Set the temperature (usually low or high) and the time (short or long cook). Then, go about your day. Seriously, forget about it. The crock pot doesn't need constant attention; it's the low-maintenance BFF of kitchen appliances.

The Aromas of Anticipation

As your home fills with the delightful scent of a home-cooked meal, you'll realize the crock pot is doing its job. It's turning those raw ingredients into a symphony of flavors. When you lift the lid, be prepared for a waft of deliciousness that'll make your taste buds do a happy dance.

Taste Test and Adjust

Before you plate up, give it a taste. Need more salt? A dash of pepper? Now's the time to tweak it to perfection. The crock pot is forgiving, so feel free to make it your own.

Serve and Enjoy

Congratulations! You've just created a masterpiece without breaking a sweat. Dish it up, savor the flavors, and relish in the fact that you've conquered the art of crock pot cooking.

Essential Features of Your Crock Pot

Temperature Settings

The crock pot's temperature settings are the secret sauce behind its magic. Typically offering low and high settings, these allow you to control the cooking process. Low and slow is perfect for tenderizing meats and melding flavors, while the high setting is handy when you need a quicker meal.

Removable Pot

Easy cleanup is a hallmark of the crock pot. The removable pot, usually made of ceramic or stoneware, can be taken out and cleaned separately. This feature not only simplifies washing but also makes serving a breeze.

Lid Seal

The lid seal ensures that the steam and flavors stay trapped inside the crock pot. This helps in retaining moisture, allowing ingredients to cook evenly and preventing the dish from drying out. A well-sealed lid also contributes to energy efficiency.

Keep-Warm Function

Say goodbye to cold dinners! The keep-warm function is a game-changer. Once your meal has finished cooking, the crock pot automatically switches to a lower temperature, keeping your food warm without overcooking it. Perfect for those unpredictable schedules.

Timer and Programmable Settings

Some crock pots come with programmable features, allowing you to set specific cook times. This is handy if you want your meal to be ready at a specific hour or if you prefer a shorter cooking time for certain recipes. It's like having a chef on autopilot.

Capacity Options

Crock pots come in various sizes to suit different needs. Whether you're cooking for one or preparing a feast for a family gathering, there's a size that fits. This adaptability makes the crock pot a versatile tool for any kitchen.

Cool-Touch Exterior

Safety first! The cool-touch exterior ensures that you can handle the crock pot without risking burns. This feature is especially beneficial if you need to move the appliance or check on your meal during the cooking process.

Indicator Lights

Simple but practical indicator lights let you know at a glance whether your crock pot is on and actively cooking. It's a small detail that adds to the user-friendly nature of the appliance.

Stylish Designs

Crock pots aren't just functional; they can be stylish, too. With a variety of designs and finishes, you can choose a crock pot that not only meets your cooking needs but also complements your kitchen decor.

Budget-Friendly Cooking

One often overlooked feature of the crock pot is its ability to make budget-friendly meals. It excels at transforming economical cuts of meat into delicious, tender dishes, making it a friend to both your schedule and your wallet.

Get ready for a delicious ride; each page is a treasure map to simple, tasty, and super-easy dishes. Let the smell of good food fill your kitchen as you discover meals that are cozy, hearty, and simple to make. Turn the pages, start the fun, and turn basic stuff into amazing meals that make everyone smile. Your crock pot is exciting; the tasty journey begins on every page!

BREAKFAST & BRUNCH RECIPES

Oats & Seeds Granola

INGREDIENTS:

- Non-stick baking spray
- Sunflower seeds – ½ C.
- Rolled oats – 5 C.
- Ground flaxseeds – 2 tbsp.
- Applesauce – ¾ C.
- Olive oil – ¼ C.
- Unsalted butter – ¼ C. melted
- Ground cinnamon – 1 tsp.
- Dates – ½ C. pitted and finely cut up
- Golden raisins – ½ C.

SERVES: 4
PER SERVING:
Calories 302,
Carbs 8g,
Fat 23g,
Protein 17g

COOK TIME: 2½ hours

DIRECTIONS:

1. Spray the pot of your Crock Pot with baking spray.
2. In the pot, place sunflower kernels, oats, flaxseeds, applesauce, oil, butter, and cinnamon and stir to incorporate.
3. Close the lid of your Crock Pot and set it on the "High" setting for 2½ hours.
4. While cooking, stir the mixture after every 30 minutes.
5. After cooking time is finished, take off the lid and shift the granola onto a large-sized baking tray.
6. Add in the dates and raisins and stir to incorporate.
7. Put it aside to cool thoroughly before serving.
8. Break the granola into pieces and enjoy.

Nutty Banana Oatmeal

INGREDIENTS:

- Steel-cut oats – 1 C.
- Ripe banana – 1, peeled and mashed
- Walnuts – ¼ C. cut up
- Flaxseeds meal – 2 tbsp.
- Water – 2 C.
- Pure vanilla extract – 1 tsp.
- Ground nutmeg – ¼ tsp.
- Unsweetened almond milk – 2 C.
- Ground cinnamon – 1 tsp.
- Ground ginger – ¼ tsp.

SERVES: 6
PER SERVING:
Calories 322,
Carbs 41.6g,
Fat 12.5g,
Protein 12.1g

COOK TIME: 8 hours

DIRECTIONS:

1. In the pot of your Crock Pot, place oats and remaining ingredients and lightly stir to incorporate.
2. Close the lid of your Crock Pot and set it on "Low" setting for 8 hours.
3. After cooking time is finished, take off the lid and stir the mixture.
4. Enjoy moderately hot.

Nutty Squash & Apple Porridge

INGREDIENTS:

- Raw almonds – ½ C. soaked for 12 hours and liquid removed
- Raw walnuts – ½ C. soaked for 12 hours and liquid removed
- Apples – 2, peeled, cored and cubed
- Medium-sized butternut squash – 1, peeled and cubed
- Applesauce – 1 tbsp.
- Ground cinnamon – 1 tsp.
- Ground ginger – ¼ tsp.
- Ground nutmeg – ¼ tsp.
- Whole milk – 1 C.

SERVES: 8

PER SERVING:
Calories 169,
Carbs 25.4g,
Fat 7.2g g,
Protein 4.8g

COOK TIME: 8 hours

DIRECTIONS:

1. Soak almonds and walnuts in a large bowl of water for around 12 hours.
2. Then, drain the nuts thoroughly.
3. In a food mixer, place nuts and pulse to form a meal-like texture.
4. In the pot of your Crock Pot, place the nut meal and remaining ingredients and lightly stir to incorporate.
5. Close the lid of your Crock Pot and set it on "Low" setting for 8 hours.
6. After cooking time is finished, take off the lid and, with a potato masher, mash the mixture slightly.
7. Enjoy moderately hot.

Sweet Potato Porridge

INGREDIENTS:

- Apple juice – 1 C. divided
- Sweet potatoes – 2 lb. peeled and cubed
- Ground allspice – ½ tsp.
- Ground cinnamon – 1 tbsp.
- Ground nutmeg – 1 tsp.
- Ground ginger – ¼ tsp.
- Pecans – ¼ C. cut up

SERVES: 8

PER SERVING:
Calories 181,
Carbs 36.7g,
Fat 3.3g,
Protein 2.3g

COOK TIME: 5 hours

DIRECTIONS:

1. In the pot of your Crock Pot, place ½ C. of apple juice and the remaining ingredients except for pecans and stir to incorporate.
2. Close the lid of your Crock Pot and set it on "Low" setting for 4-5 hours.
3. After cooking time is finished, take off the lid and stir in the remaining apple juice.
4. With a potato masher, mash the mixture thoroughly.
5. Enjoy moderately hot with the topping of pecan.

Cranberry Quinoa Porridge

INGREDIENTS:

- Coconut water – 3 C.
- Quinoa – 1 C. rinsed
- Maple syrup – 3 tsp.
- Vanilla extract – 1 tsp.
- Dried cranberries – ¼ C.
- Almonds – 2 tbsp. sliced
- Coconut flakes – 2 tbsp.

SERVES: 4

PER SERVING:
Calories 237,
Carbs 39.1g,
Fat 5.3g,
Protein 8g

DIRECTIONS:

COOK TIME: 2 hours

1. In the pot of your Crock Pot, place coconut water and remaining ingredients and stir to incorporate.
2. Close the lid of your Crock Pot and set it on the "High" setting for 2 hours.
3. After cooking time is finished, take off the lid and stir the mixture.
4. Enjoy moderately hot.

Millet Porridge

INGREDIENTS:

- Millet – 1 C.
- Fresh strawberries – 3 C. hulled and cut up
- Whole milk – 4 C.
- Maple syrup – 6 tsp.

SERVES: 4

PER SERVING:
Calories 313,
Carbs 49.1g,
Fat 8.3g,
Protein 11.3g

DIRECTIONS:

COOK TIME: 4 hours

1. In the pot of your Crock Pot, place millet and remaining ingredients and stir to incorporate.
2. Close the lid of your Crock Pot and set it on the "High" setting for 4 hours.
3. After cooking time is finished, take off the lid and stir the mixture.
4. Enjoy moderately hot.

Bulgur & Oats Porridge

INGREDIENTS:

- Bulgur – 1 C.
- Steel-cut oats – 1 C.
- Water – 6 C.
- Whole milk – 2 C.
- Honey – ½ C.
- Unrefined coconut oil – 2 tbsp.
- Vanilla extract – 1 tbsp.
- Ground cinnamon – 1 tbsp.

SERVES: 8

PER SERVING:
Calories 236,
Carbs 41.3g,
Fat 6.3g,
Protein 5.6g

DIRECTIONS:

COOK TIME: 10 hours

1. In the pot of your Crock Pot, place bulgur and remaining ingredients and stir to incorporate.
2. Close the lid of your Crock Pot and set it on "Low" setting for 8-10 hours.
3. After cooking time is finished, take off the lid and blend the mixture.
4. Enjoy moderately hot.

Barley, Quinoa & Oats Porridge

INGREDIENTS:

- Pearl barley – ¾ C.
- Steel-cut oats – ¾ C.
- Quinoa – ½ C. rinsed
- Unsweetened almond milk – 6 C.
- Coconut water – 2 C.
- Maple syrup – ¼ C.
- Vanilla extract – 1½ tsp.
- Salt – ¼ tsp.

SERVES: 10

PER SERVING:
Calories 165,
Carbs 33.5g,
Fat 3.7g,
Protein 5.2g

DIRECTIONS:

COOK TIME: 7 hours

1. In the pot of your Crock Pot, place barley and the remaining ingredients and stir to incorporate.
2. Close the lid of your Crock Pot and set it on "Low" setting for 5-7 hours.
3. After cooking time is finished, take off the lid and stir the mixture.
4. Enjoy moderately hot.

Applesauce Oats Bread

INGREDIENTS:

- Non-stick baking spray
- Yeast – 1 tbsp.
- Warm water – ¼ C.
- Rolled oats – ½ C.
- Wheat germ – ¼ C.
- Egg – 1, whisked
- Warm whole milk – 1 C.
- Applesauce – 2 tbsp.
- Olive oil – 2 tbsp.
- Whole-wheat flour – 2¾ C.

SERVES: 12

PER SERVING:
Calories 164,
Carbs 27.1g,
Fat 3.7g,
Protein 5.6g

DIRECTIONS:

COOK TIME: 3 hours

1. Set the Crock Pot on the "High" setting and let it heat thoroughly.
2. Spray an oven-proof soufflé dish with baking spray.
3. In a small bowl, mix the yeast in warm water.
4. Add in the remaining ingredients except for flour and blend to incorporate.
5. Add in flour and knead to form a sticky and smooth dough.
6. Shift the dough into a soufflé dish and cover it with a piece of heavy-duty foil.
7. Arrange a trivet in the pot of your Crock Pot and then pour in ½ C. of water.
8. Arrange the soufflé dish on top of the trivet.
9. Close the lid of your Crock Pot and set it on "Low" setting for 2½-3 hours.
10. After cooking time is finished, take off the lid and shift the bread onto a platter to cool thoroughly.
11. Divide into serving portions and enjoy.

Zucchini Bread

INGREDIENTS:

- Zucchini – 2½ C. shredded
- Salt – ½ tsp.
- Almond flour – 1 1/3 C.
- Unsweetened coconut – 2/3 C. shredded
- Swerve sweetener – ½ C.
- Whey protein powder – ¼ C.
- Baking powder – 2 tsp.
- Ground cinnamon – 2 tsp.
- Ground ginger – ½ tsp.
- Ground nutmeg – ¼ tsp.
- Large-sized eggs – 4
- Coconut oil – ¼ C. melted
- Water – ¼ C.
- Vanilla extract – ½ tsp.
- Pecans – ½ C. cut up
- Non-stick baking spray

SERVES: 10

PER SERVING:
Calories 154,
Carbs 13.7g,
Fat 12.8g,
Protein 8g

DIRECTIONS:

COOK TIME: 3 hours

1. Arrange a large-sized sieve in a sink.
2. Place the zucchini in the sieve and sprinkle with salt. Put it aside to drain for around 1 hour.
3. Squeeze out moisture from the zucchini.
4. In a large bowl, stir together almond flour, coconut, sweetener, protein powder, baking powder, and spices.
5. Add in zucchini, eggs, coconut oil, water, and vanilla extract and stir to incorporate thoroughly.
6. Fold in pecans.
7. Spray the pot of your Crock Pot with baking spray.
8. Place the mixture into the pot.
9. Close the lid of your Crock Pot and set it on "Low" setting for 2½-3 hours.
10. After cooking time is finished, take off the lid and shift the bread onto a platter to cool thoroughly.
11. Divide into serving portions and enjoy.

Veggie Omelet

INGREDIENTS:

- Non-stick baking spray
- Unsweetened almond milk – ½ C.
- Eggs – 6
- Red chili powder – 1/8 tsp.
- Garlic powder – 1/8 tsp.
- Salt and ground black pepper – as desired
- Medium-sized bell pepper – 1, seeded and thinly sliced
- Broccoli florets – 1 C.
- Small-sized onion – 1, cut up
- Fresh parsley – 2 tbsp. cut up

SERVES: 4

PER SERVING:
Calories 125,
Carbs 6.4g,
Fat 7.2g,
Protein 9.7g

COOK TIME: 2 hours

DIRECTIONS:

1. Lightly spray the pot of your Crock Pot with baking spray.
2. In a bowl, place almond milk, eggs, chili powder, garlic powder, salt, and pepper and whisk to incorporate thoroughly.
3. In the pot, stir together bell pepper, broccoli and onion.
4. Pour egg mixture on top and lightly blend to incorporate.
5. Close the lid of your Crock Pot and set it on the "High" setting for 1½-2 hours.
6. After cooking time is finished, take off the lid and move the omelet onto a serving plate.
7. Divide into serving portions and enjoy hot with the decoration of parsley.

Artichoke & Peppers Frittata

INGREDIENTS:

- Non-stick baking spray
- Eggs – 8
- Salt and ground black pepper – as desired
- Roasted red peppers – 1 (12-oz.) jar, liquid removed and cut up
- Artichoke hearts – 1 (14-oz.) can, liquid removed and cut up
- Scallion – ¼ C. cut up
- Feta cheese – 4 oz. crumbled
- Fresh parsley – 2 tbsp. cut up

SERVES: 6

PER SERVING:
Calories 107,
Carbs 9g,
Fat 7.6g,
Protein 9.7g

COOK TIME: 3 hours

DIRECTIONS:

1. Spray the pot of your Crock Pot with baking spray.
2. In a bowl, place eggs, salt, and pepper and whisk thoroughly.
3. Place red peppers, artichoke hearts, and scallion into the pot.
4. Place egg mixture over vegetables and lightly stir to incorporate.
5. Top with cheese.
6. Close the lid of your Crock Pot and set it on the "Low" setting for 2-3 hours.
7. After cooking time is finished, take off the lid and shift the frittata onto a serving plate.
8. Divide into serving portions and enjoy with the decoration of parsley.

Chicken & Veggie Frittata

INGREDIENTS:

- Non-stick baking spray
- Eggs – 8
- Salt and ground black pepper – as desired
- Cooked chicken – 1 1/3 C. finely cut up
- Bell pepper – 1½ C. seeded and cut up
- Frozen spinach – ¾ C. thawed and squeezed
- Onion – ¼ C. cut up

SERVES: 8

PER SERVING:
Calories 107,
Carbs 2.5g,
Fat 5.2g,
Protein 12.7g

COOK TIME: 3 hours

DIRECTIONS:

1. Spray the pot of your Crock Pot with baking spray.
2. In a bowl, put eggs, salt, and pepper and whisk thoroughly.
3. Place the remaining ingredients into the pot.
4. Place egg mixture over chicken mixture and lightly blend to incorporate.
5. Close the lid of the Crock Pot and set it on the "Low" setting for 2-3 hours.
6. After cooking time is finished, take off the lid and move the frittata onto a serving plate.
7. Divide into serving portions and enjoy.

Sausage Frittata

INGREDIENTS:

- Non-stick baking spray
- Pork sausage – 12 oz.
- Salsa – 1 C.
- Red chili powder – 1 tsp.
- Ground cumin – 1 tsp.
- Ground coriander – ½ tsp.
- Garlic powder – ½ tsp.
- Salt and ground black pepper – as desired
- Eggs – 10
- Unsweetened almond milk 1 C.
- Pepper Jack cheese – 1 C. shredded

SERVES: 8

PER SERVING:
Calories 294,
Carbs 3.6g,
Fat 2.6g,
Protein 18.9g

COOK TIME: 5 hours 5 minutes

DIRECTIONS:

1. Spray the pot of your Crock Pot with baking spray.
2. Heat a large-sized wok on a burner at around medium heat and cook the sausage for around 4-5 minutes.
3. Stir in the salsa and spices and take off from the burner. Put it aside to cool slightly.
4. In a bowl, put eggs and almond milk and whisk thoroughly.
5. Put in the sausage mixture and cheese and stir to incorporate.
6. Place the sausage mixture into the pot.
7. Close the lid of the Crock Pot and set it on the "Low" setting for 5 hours.
8. After cooking time is finished, take off the lid and move the frittata onto a serving plate.
9. Divide into serving portions and enjoy.

Bacon & Veggie Frittata

INGREDIENTS:

- Non-stick baking spray
- Large-sized bacon slices – 3, cut up
- Fresh mushrooms – 1 C. cut up
- Red bell pepper – ½ C. seeded and cut up
- Onion – 3 tbsp. cut up
- Large-sized kale leaves – 8, tough stalks removed and finely cut up
- Large-sized eggs – 6
- Salt and ground black pepper – as desired
- Butter – 1 tbsp. melted
- Parmesan cheese – 1 C. shredded

SERVES: 4

PER SERVING:
Calories 369,
Carbs 8.2g,
Fat 25.2g,
Protein 27.3g

DIRECTIONS:

COOK TIME: 1 hour 40 minutes

1. Heat a wok on a burner at around medium-high heat and cook bacon for around 4-5 minutes.
2. Add mushrooms, bell pepper, and onion and sauté for around 4-5 minutes.
3. Stir in kale and take off from the burner.
4. In a bowl, add eggs, salt, and black pepper and whisk to incorporate thoroughly.
5. Spray the pot of your Crock Pot with melted butter.
6. In the pot, place the veggie mixture and top with the cheese, followed by the egg mixture evenly.
7. With a wooden spoon, gently stir to combine.
8. Close the lid of the Crock Pot and set it on the "High" setting for 1½ hours.
9. After cooking time is finished, take off the lid and move the frittata onto a serving plate.
10. Divide into serving portions and enjoy.

Notes

CHICKEN & POULTRY RECIPES

Lemony Herbed Whole Chicken

INGREDIENTS:

- Non-stick baking spray
- Whole chicken – 1 (4-lb.), giblets removed
- Salt and ground black pepper – as desired
- Dried thyme – 1 tsp.
- Dried rosemary – 1 tsp.
- Dried basil – 1 tsp.
- Lemon juice – ½ C.

SERVES: 8

PER SERVING:
Calories 436,
Carbs 0.6g,
Fat 17g,
Protein 65.8gg

DIRECTIONS:

COOK TIME: 8 hours

1. Spray the pot of your Crock Pot with baking spray.
2. Rub the cavity and outer side of the chicken with salt and pepper.
3. In the pot of your Crock Pot, place chicken and sprinkle with herbs.
4. Drizzle the chicken with lemon juice.
5. Close the lid of your Crock Pot and set it on the "Low" setting for 8 hours.
6. After cooking time is finished, take off the lid and place the chicken on a chopping block for around 10 minutes.
7. Cut into serving portions and enjoy.

Sweet & Spicy Whole Chicken

INGREDIENTS:

- Non-stick baking spray
- Brown sugar – 2 tbsp.
- Paprika – 1 tbsp.
- Cayenne pepper powder – 1 tsp.
- Onion powder – ½ tsp.
- Garlic powder – ½ tsp.
- Salt and ground black pepper – as desired
- Whole chicken – 1 (5-lb.) giblets removed

SERVES: 10

PER SERVING:
Calories 437,
Carbs 1.4g,
Fat 16.9g,
Protein 65.7g

DIRECTIONS:

COOK TIME: 4 hours 5 minutes

1. Spray the pot of your Crock Pot with baking spray.
2. Roll a piece of heavy-duty foil into a ring shape and then arrange it in the pot of your Crock Pot.
3. Put brown sugar, spices, salt, and pepper into a small-sized bowl and stir to incorporate.
4. Rub the cavity and outer side of the chicken with the spice mixture.
5. Arrange the chicken on top of the foil ring.
6. Close the lid of your Crock Pot and set it on the "High" setting for 4 hours.
7. Meanwhile, preheat your oven to broiler.
8. After cooking time is finished, take off the lid and place the chicken onto a broiler pan.
9. Broil for approximately 4-5 minutes
10. Take the chicken from the oven and place on a chopping block for around 10 minutes.
11. Cut into serving portions and enjoy.

Chicken Leg Quarters & Olives

INGREDIENTS:

- Pepperoncini peppers – 12, rinsed
- Kalamata olives – 1 C. pitted and sliced
- Garlic cloves – 8, finely cut up
- Chicken legs – 3½ lb.
- Paprika – 1½ tsp.
- Salt and ground black pepper – as desired
- Lemon zest – ½ tsp. grated
- Lemon juice – ½ C.
- Sour cream – 1 C.

SERVES: 4

PER SERVING:
Calories 445,
Carbs 8.9g,
Fat 31.2g,
Protein 35.7g

DIRECTIONS:

COOK TIME: 6 hours 40 minutes

1. In the pot of your Crock Pot, place pepperoncini, followed by the olive slices, garlic, and chicken leg quarters.
2. Sprinkle with paprika, salt, pepper, and lemon zest, and then drizzle with lemon juice.
3. Close the lid of your Crock Pot and set it on "Low" setting for 6-6½ hours.
4. After cooking time is finished, take off the lid and, with a frying ladle, shift the chicken leg quarters onto a platter.
5. With a piece of heavy-duty foil, cover the chicken leg quarters to keep warm.
6. Set the Crock Pot on the "High" setting, and with a frying ladle, skim off the fat from the cooking liquid.
7. Add in sour cream, beating continuously to incorporate thoroughly.
8. Close the lid of your Crock Pot and cook for 10 minutes.
9. Pour hot sauce over the chicken and enjoy.

Creamy & Lemony Chicken Drumsticks

INGREDIENTS:

- Chicken drumsticks – 8
- Salt and ground black pepper – as desired
- Unsweetened coconut milk – 1 C.
- Fresh lemongrass stalk – 1, trimmed and cut up
- Fresh ginger – 1 (1-inch) piece, cut up
- Garlic cloves – 4, finely cut up
- Five spice powder – 1 tsp.
- Large-sized onion – 1, thinly sliced

SERVES: 8

PER SERVING:
Calories 157,
Carbs 3.9g,
Fat 9.8g,
Protein 13.7g

DIRECTIONS:

COOK TIME: 5 hours

1. Rub the drumsticks with salt and pepper.
2. Put the remaining ingredients, except for onion into a high-power mixer and process to form a smooth mixture.
3. Put drumsticks and pureed paste into a bowl and blend thoroughly.
4. In the pot of your Crock Pot, put onion slices and top with chicken alongside the paste.
5. Close the lid of the Crock Pot and set it on the "Low" setting for 4-5 hours.
6. After cooking time is finished, take off the lid and enjoy hot.

Buttered Garlicky Chicken Thighs

INGREDIENTS:

- Non-stick baking spray
- Chicken thighs – 6 (6-oz.)
- Unsalted butter – ¼ C. cut up
- Garlic cloves – 8, cut up
- Salt and ground black pepper – as desired

SERVES: 6

PER SERVING:
Calories 286,
Carbs 1.3g,
Fat 13.8g,
Protein 38.3g

COOK TIME: 6 hours

DIRECTIONS:

1. Spray the pot of your Crock Pot with baking spray.
2. In the pot, put chicken thighs.
3. Top with butter evenly and sprinkle with garlic, salt and pepper.
4. Close the lid of the Crock Pot and set it on the "Low" setting for 6 hours.
5. After cooking time is finished, take off the lid and enjoy hot.

Maple Soy Chicken Breasts

INGREDIENTS:

- Non-stick baking spray
- Low-sodium soy sauce – 1/3 C.
- Maple syrup – 1/3 C.
- Tomato paste – 2 tbsp.
- Rice vinegar – 1 tbsp.
- Sriracha – 2 tsp.
- Garlic cloves – 4, minced
- Cornstarch – 2 tbsp.
- Boneless chicken breasts – 1½ lb.

SERVES: 4

PER SERVING:
Calories 330,
Carbs 32.4g,
Fat 8.1g,
Protein 35.2g

COOK TIME: 5½ hours

DIRECTIONS:

1. Spray the pot of your Crock Pot with baking spray.
2. In a medium-sized bowl, add the soy sauce, maple syrup, tomato paste, vinegar, Sriracha, and garlic and whisk to incorporate.
3. In the pot, put chicken breasts and top with soy sauce mixture.
4. Close the lid of the Crock Pot and set it on the "Low" setting for 4-5 hours.
5. While cooking, flip the chicken breasts once halfway through.
6. After cooking time is finished, take off the lid and move the chicken breasts onto a plate.
7. Place the cornstarch into the pot with cooking liquid and whisk to incorporate.
8. Close the lid of the Crock Pot and set it on the "Low" setting for 20-30 minutes, stirring occasionally.
9. After cooking time is finished, take off the lid and pour the pan sauce over the chicken breasts.
10. Enjoy immediately.

Spiced Chicken Breasts

INGREDIENTS:

- Dried parsley – ½ tsp.
- Paprika – ½ tsp.
- Cayenne pepper – ¼ tsp.
- Garlic powder – ¼ tsp.
- Onion powder – ¼ tsp.
- Salt and ground black pepper – as desired
- Boneless chicken breasts – 4 (4-oz.)
- Butter – 1 tbsp. melted
- Chicken broth – ¼ C.

SERVES: 4

PER SERVING:
Calories 107,
Carbs 2.5g,
Fat 5.2g,
Protein 12.7g

DIRECTIONS:

COOK TIME: 4 hours

1. In a small bowl, add the parsley, spices, salt, and black pepper and blend to incorporate.
2. Rub both sides of the chicken breasts with the spice mixture evenly.
3. In the pot of your Crock Pot, place broth and butter and blend to incorporate.
4. Place the chicken breasts and coat with broth mixture.
5. Close the lid of the Crock Pot and set it on "Low" setting for 3-4 hours.
6. After cooking time is finished, take off the lid and enjoy hot.

Veggies-Stuffed Chicken Breasts

INGREDIENTS:

- Spinach – 3 C. finely cut up
- Artichoke hearts – 1 C. cut up
- Roasted red peppers – ½ C. cut up
- Black olives – ¼ C. sliced
- Feta cheese – 4 oz. crumbled
- Dried oregano – 1 tsp.
- Garlic powder – 1 tsp.
- Chicken broth – ½ C.
- Boneless chicken breasts – 2 lb.
- Salt and ground black pepper – as desired

SERVES: 6

PER SERVING:
Calories 370,
Carbs 6.2g,
at 16.1g,
Protein 48.5g

DIRECTIONS:

COOK TIME: 6 hours

1. Put vegetables, feta, oregano, and garlic powder into a bowl and stir thoroughly. Put it aside.
2. With a small-sized knife, make a deep cut in each chicken breast to make a pocket. (Be careful not to cut through the chicken).
3. Rub chicken breast with salt and pepper.
4. Stuff each chicken breast with the veggie mixture.
5. In the pot of your Crock Pot, place broth.
6. Now, place chicken breasts in the Crock Pot; the cut side should be facing up.
7. Close the lid of your Crock Pot and set it on the "Low" setting for 4-6 hours.
8. After cooking time is finished, take off the lid and enjoy hot.

Creamy Chicken & Zoodles

INGREDIENTS:

- Non-stick baking spray
- Boneless chicken tenders – 2¼ lb.
- Large-sized onion – 1, cut up
- Fresh thyme – 1 tbsp. cut up
- Garlic powder – 1 tsp.
- Salt and ground black pepper – as desired
- Large zucchinis – 4, spiralized with blade C
- Heavy cream – 1 C.
- Cheddar cheese – 1 C. shredded

SERVES: 8

PER SERVING:
Calories 282,
Carbs 7.4g,
Fat 14.6g,
Protein 31.4g

COOK TIME: 8½ hours

DIRECTIONS:

1. Spray the pot of your Crock Pot with baking spray.
2. In the pot of your Crock Pot, place chicken, onion, thyme, garlic powder, and black pepper and stir.
3. Close the lid of your Crock Pot and set it on the "Low" setting for 8½ hours.
4. After 8 hours of cooking, place zucchini over the chicken and top with cream and cheese.
5. After cooking time is finished, take off the lid and stir the chicken mixture.
6. Enjoy hot.

Spiced Pulled Chicken

INGREDIENTS:

- Non-stick baking spray
- Boneless chicken breasts – 1 lb.
- Red chili powder – 2 tsp.
- Paprika – ½ tsp.
- Ground cumin – 1½ tsp.
- Chicken broth 1½ C.

SERVES: 4

PER SERVING:
Calories 165,
Carbs 1.8g,
Fat 5.1g,
Protein 27.5g

DIRECTIONS:

COOK TIME: 8 hours

1. In the pot of your Crock Pot, place chicken breasts and remaining ingredients and blend thoroughly.
2. Close the lid of the Crock Pot and set it on the "Low" setting for 8 hours.
3. After cooking time is finished, take off the lid and transfer the breasts into a large bowl.
4. With two forks, shred the meat and mix with pan sauce.
5. Enjoy hot.

Chicken in Tomato Sauce

INGREDIENTS:

- Boneless chicken breasts – 2 lb. cut into 1-inch chunks
- Large-sized tomatoes – 2, grated
- Onion – 1, finely cut up
- Garlic clove – 1, finely cut up
- White wine – 2 C.
- Olive oil – ¼ C.
- Tomato paste – 2 tbsp.
- Allspice berries – 2
- Cinnamon stick – 1
- Salt and ground black pepper – as desired

SERVES: 6

PER SERVING:
Calories 448,
Carbs 7.4g,
Fat 19.8g,
Protein 44.8g

COOK TIME: 6 hours

DIRECTIONS:

1. In the pot of your Crock Pot, place chicken and remaining ingredients and stir to incorporate.
2. Close the lid of your Crock Pot and set it on the "High" setting for 6 hours.
3. After cooking time is finished, take off the lid and enjoy hot.

Herbed Whole Turkey

INGREDIENTS:

- Non-stick baking spray
- Whole turkey – 1 (8-lb.), giblets removed, rinsed, and pat dried
- Butter – 2 tbsp.
- Garlic – 2 tsp. minced
- Mixed dried herbs (sage, basil, thyme, oregano) – 2 tsp.
- Salt – as desired
- Fresh rosemary sprigs – 2-3
- Fresh thyme sprigs – 2-3
- Carrots – 2 C. roughly cut up
- Celery – 2 C. roughly cut up

SERVES: 14

PER SERVING:
Calories 813,
Carbs 3.7g,
Fat 25.6g,
Protein 133.3g

COOK TIME: 8 hours 5 minutes

DIRECTIONS:

1. Spray the pot of your large-sized Crock Pot with baking spray.
2. Coat the turkey with butter generously and then rub it with garlic, dry herbs, and sea salt.
3. Stuff the cavity of the turkey with fresh herbs.
4. Fold back the wings and tie the legs with kitchen twine.
5. In the pot, place the carrots and celery and arrange the turkey on top.
6. Close the lid of the Crock Pot and set it on the "High" setting for 6-7 hours.
7. Meanwhile, preheat your oven to broiler.
8. After cooking time is finished, take off the lid and shift the turkey onto a large-sized broiler pan.
9. Shift the turkey into the oven and broil for around 5 minutes.
10. Take the turkey from the oven and place it onto a platter for around 25-30 minutes before slicing.
11. Cut into serving portions and enjoy.

BBQ Mustard Turkey Legs

INGREDIENTS:
- Non-stick baking spray
- Turkey legs – 6
- Salt and ground black pepper – as desired
- BBQ sauce – 1 C.
- Dijon mustard – 2 tbsp.

SERVES: 6

PER SERVING:
Calories 533,
Carbs 3.1g,
Fat 23.9g,
Protein 69g

COOK TIME: 8 hours

DIRECTIONS:
1. Spray the pot of your Crock Pot with baking spray.
2. Rub each turkey leg with salt and pepper.
3. Put 1/3 C. of water, BBQ sauce, and mustard into a bowl and blend to incorporate thoroughly.
4. In the pot, place turkey legs and top with sauce.
5. Close the lid of your Crock Pot and set it on the "Low" setting for 7-8 hours.
6. After cooking time is finished, take off the lid and enjoy hot.

Turkey with Veggies

INGREDIENTS:
- Boneless turkey breast – 2 lb. cubed
- Fresh mushrooms – 1 C. sliced
- Zucchini – 1 C. sliced
- Garlic cloves – 4, finely cut up
- Fresh parsley – 1 C. cut up
- Tomato paste – 2 C.
- Chicken broth – 2 C.
- Salt and ground black pepper – as desired
- Lemon juice – 2 tbsp.
-

SERVES: 6

PER SERVING:
Calories 244,
Carbs 19g,
Fat 1.7g,
Protein 44.1g

DIRECTIONS:

COOK TIME: 8 hours

1. In the pot of your Crock Pot, place turkey and remaining ingredients except lemon juice and stir to combine.
2. Close the lid of your Crock Pot and set it on the "Low" setting for 8 hours.
3. After cooking time is finished, take off the lid and enjoy hot with the drizzling of lemon juice.

Buttered Turkey Breast

INGREDIENTS:

- Non-stick baking spray
- Garlic – 2 tsp. finely cut up
- Lemon pepper seasoning – 2 tsp.
- Salt and ground black pepper – as desired
- Bone-in turkey breast – 1 (5-6-lb.)
- Unsalted butter – 4 tbsp. cut up

SERVES: 8

PER SERVING:
Calories 534,
Carbs 0.6g,
Fat 26g,
Protein 60.9g

DIRECTIONS:

COOK TIME: 8 hours

1. Spray the pot of your Crock Pot with baking spray.
2. Put garlic and spices into a bowl and blend to incorporate.
3. Rub the turkey breast with the garlic mixture.
4. Place butter under the skin of the breast.
5. Arrange turkey breast in the pot.
6. Close the lid of your Crock Pot and set it on the "Low" setting for 7 hours.
7. After cooking time is finished, take off the lid and place the turkey breast onto a chopping block for around 10-15 minutes before slicing.
8. Cut into serving portions and enjoy.

Notes

BEEF, PORK & LAMB RECIPES

Beef & Spinach Curry

INGREDIENTS:

- Beef stew meat – 1¾ lb. cubed
- Heavy cream – 1 C.
- Large-sized onion – 1, quartered
- Garlic cloves – 2, finely cut up
- Curry powder – 1 tbsp.
- Salt and ground black pepper – as desired
- Fresh spinach – 4 C. cut up

SERVES: 6

PER SERVING:
Calories 332,
Carbs 4.2g,
Fat 12.9g,
Protein 41.2g

DIRECTIONS:

COOK TIME: 6¼ hours

1. In the pot of your Crock Pot, place beef cubes, cream, onion, garlic, curry powder, salt, and pepper and stir to incorporate.
2. Close the lid of your Crock Pot and set it on the "High" setting for 6 hours.
3. After cooking time is finished, take off the lid and stir in the spinach.
4. Close the lid of your Crock Pot and set it on the "High" setting for 15 minutes.
5. After cooking time is finished, take off the lid and enjoy hot.

Spiced Beef Brisket

INGREDIENTS:

- Beef brisket – 1 (4-lb.), fat removed
- Large-sized onion – 1, sliced
- Garlic cloves – 3, cut up
- Red pepper flakes – ½ tsp.
- Paprika – ½ tsp.
- Ground cumin – ½ tsp.
- Salt and ground black pepper – as desired
- Beef broth – 2 C.

SERVES: 12

PER SERVING:
Calories 353,
Carbs 2g,
Fat 11.6g,
Protein 56.3g

DIRECTIONS:

COOK TIME: 6 hours

1. In the pot of your Crock Pot, place brisket and remaining ingredients and stir to incorporate.
2. Close the lid of your Crock Pot and set it on the "Low" setting for 6 hours.
3. After cooking time is finished, take off the lid and shift the beef brisket onto a chopping block.
4. Cut beef brisket into serving portions and enjoy.

Buttered Beef Chuck Roast

INGREDIENTS:

- Large-sized onion – 1, thinly sliced
- Unsalted butter – ¼ C. melted
- Garlic – 1 tbsp. finely cut up
- Dried oregano – 1 tsp.
- Salt and ground black pepper – as desired
- Lemon juice – 2 tbsp.
- Beef chuck roast – 2 lb. cut into bite-sized pieces.

SERVES: 6

PER SERVING:
Calories 461,
Carbs 3.1g,
Fat 27.6g,
Protein 47.5g

DIRECTIONS:

COOK TIME: 10 hours

1. In the pot of your Crock Pot, put onion and remaining ingredients except for beef cubes and mix to incorporate.
2. Put in beef cubes and stir to incorporate.
3. Close the lid of the Crock Pot and set it on the "Low" setting for 8-10 hours.
4. After cooking time is finished, take off the lid and enjoy hot.

Herb Braised Beef Shanks

INGREDIENTS:

- Unsalted butter – 3 tbsp.
- Beef shanks – 5 (1-lb.), fat removed
- Salt and ground black pepper – as desired
- Large-sized onion – 1, cut up
- Garlic cloves – 10, finely cut up
- Tomato paste – 2 tbsp.
- Fresh rosemary sprigs – 4
- Fresh thyme sprigs – 4
- Beef broth – 2 C.

SERVES: 10

PER SERVING:
Calories 513,
Carbs 3.2g,
Fat 18.9g,
Protein 77.9g

DIRECTIONS:

COOK TIME: 8 hours 10 minutes

1. In a large-sized wok, melt butter on a burner at around medium-high heat.
2. Cook beef shanks with salt and pepper on both sides for around 4-5 minutes.
3. Move the beef shanks into the pot of your Crock Pot.
4. Put onion into the same wok and sauté for around 3-4 minutes.
5. Add in garlic and sauté for around 1 minute.
6. Place onion mixture over beef shanks, followed by tomato paste.
7. With a kitchen string, tie the herb sprigs.
8. Arrange tied sprigs over tomato paste and pour broth on top.
9. Close the lid of your Crock Pot and set it on the "Low" setting for 8 hours.
10. After cooking time is finished, take off the lid and enjoy hot.

Sweet & Zesty Beef Shoulder

INGREDIENTS:

- Unsalted butter – ¼ C.
- Beef shoulder roast – 8 lb. fat removed
- Salt and ground black pepper – as desired
- Medium-sized onion – 1, cut up
- Garlic cloves – 4, finely cut up
- Dijon mustard – 1 tbsp.
- Balsamic vinegar – 2 tbsp.
- Lemon juice – 2 tbsp.
- White sugar – 2 tbsp.

SERVES: 14

PER SERVING:
Calories 518,
Carbs 3.1g,
Fat 33.1g,
Protein 48.4g

COOK TIME: 9 hours 10 minutes

DIRECTIONS:

1. Melt butter into a large-sized wok on the burner at around medium-high heat.
2. Cook beef with salt and pepper on both sides for around 1-2 minutes.
3. Place the beef into the pot of your Crock Pot.
4. Put onion into same wok and sauté for around 2-3 minutes.
5. Place onion over beef.
6. In a bowl, blend to incorporate the remaining ingredients.
7. Pour the sauce over the beef.
8. Close the lid of the Crock Pot and set it on the "Low" setting for 9 hours.
9. After cooking time is finished, take off the lid and move the beef onto a chopping block.
10. Shift the sauce into a small saucepan on a burner at around medium-high heat.
11. Cook for around 5 minutes or until desired thickness.
12. Cut beef shoulder into serving portions.
13. Pour sauce over beef slices and enjoy.

Spiced Pork Roast

INGREDIENTS:

- Garlic cloves – 4, finely cut up
- Fresh ginger – 1 tsp. finely grated
- Fish sauce – 1 tbsp.
- Soy sauce – 1 tbsp.
- Paprika – 2 tsp.
- Ground cumin – 1 tsp.
- Ground turmeric – 1 tsp.
- Boneless pork chops – 2 lb.
- Medium-sized onions – 2, cut up
- Winter squash – 1 lb. peeled and cubed

SERVES: 6

PER SERVING:
Calories 269,
Carbs 1.4g,
Fat 17.5g,
Protein 48.1g

COOK TIME: 8 hours

DIRECTIONS:

1. Rub the pork with herbs and spices.
2. In the pot of your Crock Pot, place half of the onion and top with pork roast, followed by the remaining onion.
3. Pour broth on top.
4. Close the lid of your Crock Pot and set it on "Low" setting for 6-8 hours.
5. After cooking time is finished, take off the lid and place the pork roast onto a chopping block.
6. Cut pork roast into serving portions and enjoy.

Braised Pork Shoulder

INGREDIENTS:

- Olive oil – 2 tbsp.
- Pork shoulder – 3 lb.
- Salt and ground black pepper – as desired
- Medium-sized onion – 1, cut up
- Celery stalk – 1, cut up
- Garlic cloves – 2, finely cut up
- Tomatoes – 2 C. finely cut up
- Chicken broth – ½ C.
- Lemon juice – 2 tbsp.

SERVES: 8

PER SERVING:
Calories 545,
Carbs 3.5g,
Fat 40.1g,
Protein 40.5g

DIRECTIONS:

COOK TIME: 8 hours 10 minutes

1. Melt oil into a large-sized wok on a burner at around medium-high heat.
2. Put the pork shoulder into the pot of your Crock Pot and top it with onion, celery, garlic, and tomatoes.
3. Pour broth and lemon juice on top.
4. Close the lid of your Crock Pot and set it on the "Low" setting for 8 hours.
5. After cooking time is finished, take off the lid and place the pork shoulder onto a chopping block.
6. Cut pork shoulder into serving portions and enjoy.

Garlicky Pulled Pork

INGREDIENTS:

- Medium-sized onion – 1, thinly sliced
- Garlic cloves – 4, finely cut up
- Lemongrass – 3 tbsp. finely cut up
- Balsamic vinegar – 1 tbsp.
- Olive oil – 3 tbsp.
- Salt and ground black pepper – as desired
- Pork butt – 3 lb. fat removed
- Unsweetened coconut milk – 1 C.

SERVES: 8

PER SERVING:
Calories 445,
Carbs 3.9g,
Fat 23.8g,
Protein 53.9g

DIRECTIONS:

COOK TIME: 8 hours

1. Put garlic, lemongrass, vinegar, oil, and seasoning into a large bowl and blend to incorporate.
2. Rub the pork butt with the garlic mixture.
3. In the pot of your Crock Pot, place onion slices and top with pork butt.
4. Cover the Crock Pot and put it aside to marinate for at least 8 hours.
5. Take off the lid and pour coconut milk on top.
6. Close the lid of your Crock Pot and set it on the "Low" setting for 8 hours.
7. After cooking time is finished, take off the lid and move the pork butt onto a chopping block.
8. Cut pork butt into serving portions and enjoy.

Soy Sauce Braised Pork Tenderloin

INGREDIENTS:

- Pork tenderloin – 3 lb.
- Dry onion soup mix – 1 envelope
- Salt and ground black pepper – as desired
- Soy sauce – 3 tbsp.
- Chicken broth – 1¾ C.

SERVES: 10

PER SERVING:
Calories 211,
Carbs 2.3g,
Fat 5g,
Protein 37g

COOK TIME: 8 hours

DIRECTIONS:

1. In the pot of your Crock Pot, place pork and remaining ingredients and stir to incorporate.
2. Close the lid of your Crock Pot and set it on the "Low" setting for 8 hours.
3. After cooking time is finished, take off the lid and place the pork tenderloin onto a chopping block.
4. Divide into serving portions and enjoy.

Pork Chops with Zucchini

INGREDIENTS:

- Coconut oil – 1 tbsp.
- Garlic cloves – 2, finely cut up
- Boneless pork chops – 5 (4-oz.)
- Salt and ground black pepper – as desired
- Large-sized zucchini – 1, cubed
- Lemons – 2, sliced
- Red pepper flakes – 1 tsp.

SERVES: 5

PER SERVING:
Calories 206,
Carbs 4.9g,
Fat 7g,
Protein 30.8g

COOK TIME: 5 hours 5 minutes

DIRECTIONS:

1. Heat oil into a large-sized wok on a burner at around medium-high heat.
2. Cook the garlic for around 1 minute.
3. Add in chops and cook for 1-2 minutes on both sides.
4. Place the chops mixture into the pot of your Crock Pot.
5. Place cubed zucchini over chops evenly, followed by lemon slices.
6. Sprinkle with red pepper flakes, salt and pepper.
7. Close the lid of your Crock Pot and set it on the "High" setting for 5 hours.
8. After cooking time is finished, take off the lid and enjoy hot.

Garlicky Lamb Shoulder

INGREDIENTS:

- Bone-in lamb shoulder – 3¼ lb. fat removed
- Medium-sized onions – 2, thinly sliced
- Garlic cloves – 5-6, cut up
- Beef broth – ¼ C.
- Olive oil – ¼ C.
- Dried thyme – 1 tbsp.
- Salt and ground black pepper – as desired

SERVES: 8

PER SERVING:
Calories 413,
Carbs 3.4g,
Fat 19.9g,
Protein 52.3g

DIRECTIONS:

COOK TIME: 5 hours 10 minutes

1. Heat a large-sized cast-iron wok on a burner at around medium-high heat.
2. Sear the lamb shoulder for around 4-5 minutes on both sides.
3. Take off from the burner.
4. In the pot of your Crock Pot, place the onion slices and garlic evenly and arrange the lamb shoulder on top.
5. Place the remaining ingredients on top.
6. Close the lid of your Crock Pot and set it on the "High" setting for 4-5 hours.
7. After cooking time is finished, take off the lid and, with a frying ladle, move the lamb shoulder onto a platter.
8. Cut the lamb shoulder into serving portions and enjoy with the topping of pan sauce.

Lamb Shanks with Potatoes

INGREDIENTS:

- Lamb shanks – 4
- Salt and ground black pepper – as desired
- Olive oil – 1 tbsp.
- Baby potatoes – 1 lb. halved
- Kalamata olives – 1 C.
- Sun-dried tomatoes – 1 – 3-oz. jar
- Chicken broth – 1 C.
- Lemon juice – 3 tbsp.
- Dried oregano – 1 tsp.
- Dried rosemary – 1 tsp.
- Dried basil – 1 tsp.
- Onion powder – 1 tsp.

SERVES: 4

PER SERVING:
Calories 696,
Carbs 22.5g,
Fat 28.6g,
Protein 83.5g

DIRECTIONS:

COOK TIME: 8 hours 5 minutes

1. Rub the lamb shanks with salt and pepper.
2. Heat the olive oil into a large-sized heavy-bottomed wok on a burner at around medium-high heat.
3. Sear the lamb shanks for around 4-5 minutes.
4. Take off from the burner.
5. In the pot of your Crock Pot, place the potatoes, olives, sun-dried tomatoes, salt and pepper.
6. Place the lamb on top and sprinkle with dried herbs and onion powder.
7. Close the lid of your Crock Pot and set it on the "Low" setting for 8 hours.
8. After cooking time is finished, take off the lid and enjoy hot.

Lamb & Squash Curry

INGREDIENTS:

- Garlic cloves – 4, finely cut up
- Fresh ginger – 1 tsp. finely grated
- Fish sauce – 1 tbsp.
- Soy sauce – 1 tbsp.
- Paprika – 2 tsp.
- Ground cumin – 1 tsp.
- Ground turmeric – 1 tsp.
- Beef stew meat – 2 lb. cubed
- Medium-sized onions – 2, cut up
- Winter squash – 1 lb. peeled and cubed

SERVES: 8

PER SERVING:
Calories 272,
Carbs 13.3g,
Fat 5.7g,
Protein 41.2g

COOK TIME: 6 hours

DIRECTIONS:

1. Put garlic, ginger, fish sauce, soy sauce, and spices into a bowl and stir to incorporate.
2. In the pot of your Crock Pot, place lamb cubes and top with the spice mixture.
3. Place onion on top evenly, followed by squash cubes.
4. Close the lid of your Crock Pot and set it on the "Low" setting for 7-8 hours.
5. After cooking time is finished, take off the lid and enjoy hot.

Lamb Meatballs in Tomato Gravy

INGREDIENTS:

- Non-stick baking spray
- Bacon slices – 2, cut up
- Onion – 1, quartered
- Garlic cloves – 2, peeled
- Ground lamb – 2 lb.
- Egg – 1
- Fresh cilantro – 1 tbsp.
- Fresh parsley – 2 tbsp.
- Salt and ground black pepper – as desired
- Diced tomatoes – 2 (14-oz.) cans with juice

SERVES: 8

PER SERVING:
Calories 305,
Carbs 5.8g,
Fat 11.6g,
Protein 42.4g

COOK TIME: 8 hours

DIRECTIONS:

1. Spray the pot of your Crock Pot with baking spray.
2. In a food processor, put the bacon, onion, and garlic, and process them to cut up finely.
3. Add ground lamb, egg, herbs, salt, and black pepper and pulse until smooth.
4. Make small-sized balls from the mixture.
5. In the pot, place the meatballs and top with tomatoes.
6. Close the lid of the Crock Pot and set it on the "Low" setting for 6-8 hours.
7. After cooking time is finished, take off the lid and enjoy hot.

Cheesy Beef Lasagna

INGREDIENTS:

- Lean ground beef – 1 lb.
- Medium-sized onion – 1, cut up
- Pasta sauce – 1 (24-oz.) jar
- Fresh basil leaves – 3-5, cut up
- Salt – as desired
- Mozzarella cheese – 2 C. shredded and divided
- Parmesan cheese – 1 C. shredded
- Ricotta cheese – 15 oz.
- Uncooked lasagna noodles – 15

SERVES: 6

PER SERVING:
Calories 582,
Carbs 52g,
Fat 19.6g,
Protein 47.4g

COOK TIME: 4 hours

DIRECTIONS:

1. Heat a non-stick wok on a burner at around medium heat.
2. Cook the beef and onion for around 8-10 minutes.
3. Drain the grease from the wok.
4. Put pasta sauce, basil, and salt into the same wok and blend to incorporate.
5. Remove the wok from the burner and put it aside.
6. Put 1 C. of mozzarella, Parmesan, and ricotta cheese in a bowl and stir to incorporate.
7. In the pot of your Crock Pot, put ¼ of the beef mixture and arrange 5 noodles on top, breaking them to fit in the pot.
8. Place half of the cheese mixture on top of the noodles.
9. Repeat the layer twice, ending with ¼ of the beef mixture.
10. Close the lid of your Crock Pot and set it on the "Low" setting for 4-6 hours.
11. In the last 20 minutes of cooking, sprinkle the lasagna with the remaining mozzarella cheese.
12. After cooking time is finished, take off the lid and enjoy hot.

Notes

FISH & SEAFOOD RECIPES

Teriyaki Salmon

INGREDIENTS:

SERVES: 4

PER SERVING:
Calories 236,
Carbs 12.7g,
Fat 10.1g,
Protein 24.1g

- Teriyaki sauce – 1/3 C.
- Soy sauce – ¼ C.
- Rice vinegar – 1 tbsp.
- Sesame oil – 1 tbsp.
- Brown sugar – 1/3 C.
- Garlic cloves – 3, finely cut up
- Fresh ginger – 1 tbsp. finely cut up
- Salmon fillet – 1½ lb.
- Salt and ground black pepper – as desired
- Sesame seeds – 1 tbsp. toasted

DIRECTIONS:

COOK TIME: 2 hours

1. Place teriyaki sauce, soy sauce, vinegar, sesame oil, brown sugar, garlic, and ginger into a bowl and whisk to incorporate.
2. Rub the salmon with salt and pepper.
3. In the pot of your Crock Pot, put salmon fillets and top with sauce mixture.
4. Close the lid of the Crock Pot and set it on the "Low" setting for 2 hours.
5. After cooking time is finished, take off the lid and enjoy hot with the decoration of sesame seeds.

Salmon in Wine Sauce

INGREDIENTS:

SERVES: 6

PER SERVING:
Calories 286,
Carbs 4.1g,
Fat 10.6g,
Protein 33.8g

- Water – 2 C.
- Dry white wine – 1 C.
- Shallot – 1, thinly sliced
- Lemon – 1, thinly sliced
- Fresh dill – ¼ C. cut up
- Boneless salmon fillets – 6 (4-oz.)
- Salt and ground black pepper – as desired

DIRECTIONS:

COOK TIME: 1 hour

1. In the pot of your Crock Pot, put water, wine, shallot, lemon, and dill and stir to incorporate.
2. Arrange salmon fillets on top, skin side down.
3. Sprinkle with salt and pepper.
4. Close the lid of the Crock Pot and set it on the "Low" setting for 1 hour.
5. After cooking time is finished, take off the lid and enjoy hot.

Salmon with Mushrooms

INGREDIENTS:

- Non-stick baking spray
- Boneless salmon fillets – 2 (4-oz.)
- Scallions – ½ C. thinly sliced
- Fresh mushrooms – 1 C. sliced
- Salt and ground black pepper – as desired
- Fish broth – 3 C.

SERVES: 2

PER SERVING:
Calories 225,
Carbs 31.5g,
Fat 10g,
Protein 54.7g

COOK TIME: 2 hours

DIRECTIONS:

1. In the pot of your Crock Pot, put salmon and the remaining ingredients and stir to incorporate.
2. Close the lid of the Crock Pot and set it on the "Low" setting for 1-2 hours.
3. After cooking time is finished, take off the lid and enjoy hot.

Lemony Thyme Halibut

INGREDIENTS:

- Non-stick baking spray
- Fresh parsley – ¾ C. cut up
- Garlic cloves – 2, finely cut up
- Lime juice – 2-3 tbsp.
- Olive oil – 1 tbsp.
- Salt – as desired
- Halibut fillets – 1 lb.

SERVES: 4

PER SERVING:
Calories 184,
Carbs 0.7g,
Fat 10.5g,
Protein 22.2g

COOK TIME: 2½ hours

DIRECTIONS:

1. Spray the pot of your Crock Pot with baking spray.
2. Put parsley and the remaining ingredients, except for the salmon fillets, into a medium bowl and stir thoroughly.
3. In the pot of your Crock Pot, put fish fillets and top with the garlic mixture.
4. Close the lid of the Crock Pot and set it on the "Low" setting for 2-2½ hours.
5. After cooking time is finished, take off the lid and enjoy hot.

Buttered Tilapia

INGREDIENTS:

- Boneless tilapia fillets – 4 (4-oz.)
- Salt and ground black pepper – as desired
- Unsalted butter – 2 tbsp. cubed
- Lemon – 1, cut into slices

SERVES: 4

PER SERVING:
Calories 169,
Carbs 0.4g,
Fat 7.1g,
Protein 26.5g

DIRECTIONS:

COOK TIME: 1½ hours

1. In the pot of your Crock Pot, put tilapia fillets and sprinkle with salt and pepper.
2. Top with butter, followed by the lemon.
3. Close the lid of the Crock Pot and set it on the "Low" setting for 1½ hours.
4. After cooking time is finished, take off the lid and enjoy hot.

Haddock Pie

INGREDIENTS:

- Whole milk –2/3 C.
- Cream cheese – ½ C.
- Haddock – 1 lb. cut into bite-sized pieces
- Frozen green peas – 10 oz.
- Frozen corn – 10 oz.
- Salt and ground black pepper – as desired
- Non-stick baking spray
- Cheddar cheese – ½ C. shredded
- Breadcrumb – ¼ C.

SERVES: 6

PER SERVING:
Calories 475,
Carbs 60.3g,
Fat 13.9g,
Protein 34.4g

DIRECTIONS:

COOK TIME: 2 hours 10 minutes

1. Put milk and cream cheese into a bowl and stir to incorporate thoroughly.
2. Put haddock pieces, peas, corn, salt, and pepper into another bowl and stir to incorporate.
3. Spray the pot of your Crock Pot with baking spray.
4. In the pot, put the haddock mixture and top with the milk mixture.
5. Close the lid of the Crock Pot and set it on the "High" setting for 2 hours.
6. Meanwhile, set your oven to 400 °F.
7. Put cheddar cheese and breadcrumbs into a bowl and blend to incorporate.
8. After cooking time is finished, take off the lid and shift the pot onto a counter.
9. Sprinkle the top of the pie with the cheddar mixture.
10. Bake for around 10 minutes.
11. Remove it from the oven and put it aside for around 5 minutes before serving.

Shrimp Curry

INGREDIENTS:

- Unsweetened coconut milk – 1 C.
- Onion – 1, cut up
- Bell pepper – 1, seeded and thinly sliced
- Celery – ½ C. cut up
- Tomatoes – 4 C. cut up
- Red curry paste – 2 tbsp.
- Fresh basil – 2 tbsp. cut up
- Salt and ground black pepper – as desired
- Shrimp – 1 lb. peeled and deveined
- Fresh parsley – ¼ C. cut up

SERVES: 4

PER SERVING:
Calories 311,
Carbs 17.2g,
Fat 13g,
Protein 29g

COOK TIME: 5 hours 40 minutes

DIRECTIONS:

1. In the pot of your Crock Pot, put coconut milk and the remaining ingredients except for shrimp and parsley and stir to incorporate.
2. Close the lid of the Crock Pot and set it on the "Low" setting for 5 hours.
3. After cooking time is finished, take off the lid and stir in the shrimp.
4. Close the lid of the Crock Pot and set it on the "Low" setting for 40 minutes.
5. After cooking time is finished, take off the lid and enjoy hot with the decoration of parsley.

Shrimp with Pasta

INGREDIENTS:

- Uncooked pasta – 1½ C.
- Whole peeled tomatoes – 1 (14½-oz.) can, cut up
- Tomato paste – 1 (6-oz.) can
- Fresh parsley – 2 tbsp. finely cut up
- Garlic clove – 1, finely cut up
- Dried oregano – 1 tsp.
- Dried basil – 1 tsp.
- Seasoned salt – 1 tsp.
- Cooked shrimp – 1 lb.
- Salt and ground black pepper – as desired
- Parmesan cheese – ¼ C. shredded

SERVES: 4

PER SERVING:
Calories 295,
Carbs 34.6g,
Fat 3.8g,
Protein 33.1g

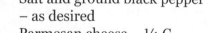
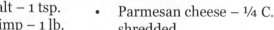

COOK TIME: 7¼ hours

DIRECTIONS:

1. In the pot of your Crock Pot, put pasta and remaining ingredients except for shrimp and Parmesan and stir to incorporate.
2. Close the lid of the Crock Pot and set it on the "Low" setting for 6-7 hours.
3. After cooking time is finished, take off the lid and blend in the cooked shrimp.
4. Sprinkle with parmesan cheese.
5. Again, close the lid of the Crock Pot and set it on the "High" setting for 15 minutes.
6. After cooking time is finished, take off the lid and enjoy hot.

Octopus with Potatoes

INGREDIENTS:

- Octopus – 1½ lb.
- Fingerling potatoes – 6
- Lemon – ½, cut into slices
- Salt and ground black pepper – as desired
- Water – as desired
- Olive oil – 3 tbsp.
- Capers – 3 tbsp.

SERVES: 4
PER SERVING:
Calories 308,
Carbs 18.5g,
Fat 12.3g,
Protein 30.6g

COOK TIME: 6 hours

DIRECTIONS:

1. Remove the beak, eyes, and any other parts of the octopus.
2. Rinse the inside and outside of the octopus head and tentacles.
3. Cut off the head of the octopus at its base.
4. Using a pair of tongs, dip the octopus into a pan of boiling water for around 10-15 seconds.
5. Now, put the octopus in the pot of your Crock Pot.
6. Place in the potatoes, lemon slices, salt, pepper, and enough water to cover.
7. Close the lid of the Crock Pot and set it on the "High" setting for 5-6 hours.
8. After cooking time is finished, take off the lid and drain the octopus into a colander.
9. With a frying ladle, move the potatoes onto a platter.
10. With paper towels, pat dry the potatoes and cut them into thin slices.
11. Cut the octopus into thin slices.
12. Put octopus, potatoes, oil, capers, salt, and pepper into a large bowl and blend to incorporate.
13. Enjoy immediately.

Seafood Jambalaya

INGREDIENTS:

- Unsalted butter – 1 tsp.
- Bacon slices – 2, cut up.
- Sausage links – 2, sliced
- Onion – 1 C. cut up
- Celery – ¾ C. cut up
- Garlic – ½ tsp. finely cut up
- Canned diced tomatoes – 2 C.
- Long-grain white rice – 1½ C. rinsed
- Cajun seasoning – 1 tbsp.
- Dried oregano – 1 tsp.
- Dried thyme – ½ tsp.

- Cayenne pepper powder – ½ tsp.
- Salt and ground black pepper – as desired
- Chicken broth – 3 C.
- Catfish – 8 oz. cubed
- Shrimp – 8 oz. peeled and deveined

SERVES: 6
PER SERVING:
Calories 452,
Carbs 46.2g,
Fat 15.6g,
Protein 29.3g

COOK TIME: 5 hours 10 minutes

DIRECTIONS:

1. Heat a large-sized non-stick wok on a burner at around medium heat.
2. Cook the bacon for around 4-5 minutes.
3. Put in sausage slices and cook for around 4-5 minutes.
4. With a frying ladle, move the bacon and sausage slices into the pot of your Crock Pot.
5. Put in remaining ingredients except for seafood and lightly stir to incorporate.
6. Close the lid of the Crock Pot and set it on the "Low" setting for 4 hours.
7. After cooking time is finished, take off the lid and stir in the seafood.
8. Close the lid of the Crock Pot and set it on the "High" setting for 40-60 minutes.
9. After cooking time is finished, take off the lid and enjoy hot.

SOUP, STEWS & CHILIES RECIPES

Cheesy Tomato Soup

INGREDIENTS:

- Olive oil – 1 tbsp.
- Carrot – 1 C. peeled and finely cut up
- Celery – 1 C. finely cut up
- Onion – 1 C. finely cut up
- Whole plum tomatoes – 1 (28-oz.) can, crushed with juice
- Fresh basil – ¼ C. cut up
- Vegetable broth – 3½ C.
- Bay leaf – 1
- Salt and ground black pepper – as desired

SERVES: 6

PER SERVING:
Calories 311,
Carbs 15.7g,
Fat 25.8g,
Protein 8.2g

- Unsalted butter – 2 tbsp.
- Whole-wheat flour – 2 tbsp.
- Warm coconut milk – 1¾ C.
- Pecorino Romano cheese – 1/3 C. grated

COOK TIME: 6½ hours

DIRECTIONS:

1. Heat oil into a medium-sized wok on a burner at around medium heat.
2. Cook the carrots, celery, and onion for around 5-6 minutes.
3. Place the carrot mixture into the pot of your Crock Pot.
4. Put in tomatoes, basil, broth, bay leaf, salt, and pepper and blend to incorporate.
5. Close the lid of the Crock Pot and set it on the "Low" setting for 6 hours.
6. After cooking time is finished, take off the lid and let the soup cool slightly.
7. Place the soup into a mixer in batches and process to form a smooth mixture.
8. Return the soup into the pot of your Crock Pot.
9. Melt butter into a small-sized saucepan on a burner at around low heat.
10. Put in the flour and stir to form a smooth mixture.
11. Cook for around 1-2 minutes, mixing all the time.
12. Put in 1 C. of hot soup and blend thoroughly.
13. Blend in warm milk and take off from the burner.
14. Add the flour mixture and cheese into the pot with soup and stir thoroughly.
15. Close the lid of the Crock Pot and set it on the "Low" setting for 15-20 minutes.
16. After cooking time is finished, take off the lid and enjoy hot.

Beans, Pasta & Spinach Soup

INGREDIENTS:

- Onions – 2 C. cut up
- Celery – 1 C. cut up
- Carrots – 1 C. peeled and cut up
- Chicken broth – 6 C.
- Italian seasoning – 4 tsp.
- Salt – as desired
- Cooked whole-wheat rotini pasta – 4 C.
- White beans – 1 – (15-oz.) can, liquid removed
- Fresh baby spinach – 4 C.
- Fresh basil – 4 tbsp. cut up and divided
- Olive oil – 2 tbsp.
- Parmigiano Reggiano cheese – ½ C. grated

SERVES: 6

PER SERVING:
Calories 514,
Carbs 82.1g,
Fat 9g,
Protein 28g

COOK TIME: 8 hours

DIRECTIONS:

1. In the pot of your Crock Pot, put in the onions, celery, carrots, Italian seasoning, and salt and stir to incorporate.
2. Close the lid of the Crock Pot and set it on the "Low" setting for 7¼ hours.
3. After cooking time is finished, take off the lid and stir in the pasta, beans, spinach, and 2 tablespoons of basil.
4. Close the lid of the Crock Pot and set it on the "Low" setting for 45 minutes.
5. After cooking time is finished, take off the lid and pour the soup into serving bowls.
6. Drizzle each with oil and enjoy with the decoration of cheese and remaining basil.

Chicken & Rice Soup

INGREDIENTS:

- Non-stick baking spray
- Boneless chicken breasts – 1½ lb.
- Long-grain white rice – ¾ C.
- Large-sized carrots – 2, peeled and cut into slices
- Medium-sized onion – 1, cut up
- celery stalk – 1, cut up
- Salt and ground black pepper – as desired
- Chicken broth – 6 C.
- Unsalted butter – 2 tbsp. melted

- All-purpose flour – 2 tbsp.
- Eggs – 2
- Lemon juice – ¼ C.

SERVES: 6

PER SERVING:
Calories 319,
Carbs 18.5g,
Fat 10g,
Protein 30.8g

COOK TIME: 6 hours 20 minutes

DIRECTIONS:

1. In the pot of your Crock Pot, put chicken breasts, rice, carrots, onion, celery, salt, pepper, and broth and stir to incorporate.
2. Close the lid of the Crock Pot and set it on the "Low" setting for 4-6 hours.
3. After cooking time is finished, take off the lid and, with a frying ladle, move the chicken breasts onto a plate.
4. Put butter and flour into a bowl and whisk to form a smooth mixture.
5. Put about 1 C. of hot soup in the bowl of the flour mixture and whisk to form a smooth mixture.
6. Put the flour mixture into the Crock Pot with the remaining soup and blend to incorporate.
7. Put in lemon juice and blend to incorporate.
8. Put eggs into a bowl and whisk until frothy.
9. Put 1 tbsp. of the hot soup into the bowl of whisked eggs and whisk thoroughly.
10. Repeat this process 3 times.
11. Put the egg mixture into the Crock Pot with the remaining soup and stir to incorporate.
12. With 2 forks, shred the meat of the chicken breasts.
13. In the soup, put the shredded meat and blend to incorporate.
14. Again, close the lid of the Crock Pot and set it on the "High" setting for 15-20 minutes.
15. After cooking time is finished, take off the lid and enjoy hot.

Salmon, Potato & Corn Soup

INGREDIENTS:

- Creamed corn – 1 (15-oz.) can
- Corn – 8 oz. frozen
- Red potatoes – 8 oz. cut into ½-inch chunks
- Small-sized onion – 1, cut up
- Medium-sized bell pepper – 1, seeded and cut up
- Jalapeño pepper – 1, seeded and cut up
- Fish broth – 2 C.
- Old bay seasoning – 1 tsp.
- Salmon – 2 (5-oz.) cans, liquid removed
- Half-and-half – 1 C.
- Hot sauce – 3-5 dashes
- Cooked bacon slices – 4-6, crumbled

SERVES: 6

PER SERVING:
Calories 285,
Carbs 30.9g,
Fat 10.6g,
Protein 20.2g

COOK TIME: 8½ hours

DIRECTIONS:

1. Put corn, creamed corn, potatoes, onions, red peppers, jalapeno peppers, Chicken broth, and seafood seasoning into the pot of your Crock Pot.
2. Close the lid of the Crock Pot and set it on the "Low" setting for 7-8 hours.
3. After cooking time is finished, take off the lid and shift half of the mixture into a pan.
4. With an immersion blender, blend to form a smooth mixture.
5. Return the pureed soup into the pot with salmon, half-and-half, and hot sauce and blend to incorporate.
6. Close the lid of the Crock Pot and set it on the "Low" setting for 30 minutes.
7. After cooking time is finished, take off the lid and enjoy hot with a decoration of bacon.

Beef Meatballs & Zoodles Soup

INGREDIENTS:

For the Meatballs:
- Lean ground beef – 2 lb.
- Garlic cloves – 4, finely cut up
- Fresh parsley – ¼ C. cut up
- Parmesan cheese – ½ C. grated
- Egg – 1, whisked
- Dried oregano – 1 tsp.
- Dried rosemary – 1 tsp.
- Salt and ground black pepper – as desired
- Coconut oil – 2 tbsp.

For the Soup:
- Celery stalk – 1, cut up
- Small-sized onion – 1, cut up
- Small-sized carrot – 1, peeled and cut up
- Large-sized tomato – 1, finely cut up
- Large zucchinis – 3, spiralized with blade C
- Salt and ground black pepper – as desired
- Beef broth – 7 C.

SERVES: 12

PER SERVING:
Calories 241,
Carbs 5.7g,
Fat 10.5g,
Protein 3.6g

COOK TIME: 6 hours 10 minutes

DIRECTIONS:
1. For the meatballs: in a large-sized bowl, put ground beef and remaining ingredients except coconut oil and blend to incorporate thoroughly.
2. Shape the mixture into small-sized balls.
3. Heat oil in a large-sized wok on a burner at around medium-high heat.
4. In 2 batches, put in meatballs and cook for around 4-5 minutes.
5. Take off the meatballs from the burner.
6. In the pot of your Crock Pot, put celery, onion, carrot, and tomato.
7. Arrange zucchini noodles over vegetables and sprinkle with salt and pepper.
8. Pour broth over vegetables.
9. Carefully put in meatballs.
10. Close the lid of the Crock Pot and set it on the "Low" setting for 6 hours.
11. After cooking time is finished, take off the lid and enjoy hot.

Sweet Potato and Kale Stew

INGREDIENTS:
- Diced tomatoes – 1 (28-oz.) can, with juices
- Fresh cilantro leaves – 1 C.
- Garlic cloves – 3, halved
- Chunky peanut butter – ½ C.
- Ground cumin – 2 tsp.
- Ground cinnamon – ½ tsp.
- Paprika – ¼ tsp.
- Salt – 1 tsp.
- Sweet potatoes – 3½ lb. peeled and cut into 1-inch pieces

SERVES: 8

PER SERVING:
Calories 385,
Carbs 70.5g,
Fat 8.8g,
Protein 10g

- Water – 1 C.
- Fresh kale – 8 C. tough ribs removed and cut up.

COOK TIME: 8 hours

DIRECTIONS:
1. Put tomatoes, cilantro, garlic, peanut butter, spices, and salt into a food mixer and process to form a puree.
2. Place the pureed mixture into the pot of your Crock Pot and stir in the sweet potatoes and water.
3. Close the lid of the Crock Pot and set it on the "Low" setting for 8 hours.
4. In the last 30 minutes of cooking, stir in the kale.
5. After cooking time is finished, take off the lid and enjoy hot.

Turkey & Spinach Stew

INGREDIENTS:

- Olive oil – 2 tbsp. divided
- Boneless turkey breast – 1¼ lb. cubed
- Garlic powder – 1 tsp.
- Salt and ground black pepper – as desired
- Small-sized onion – 1, cut up
- Dried thyme – ½ tsp.
- Dried oregano – ½ tsp.
- Carrot – ½ C. peeled and cut up
- Celery stalk – 1, cut up
- Fresh spinach – 5 C. cut up
- Tomatoes – 1 C. finely cut up
- Chicken broth – 1½ C.
- Lemon juice – 2 tbsp.

SERVES: 4

PER SERVING:
Calories 239,
Carbs 7.5g,
Fat 8g,
Protein 37.9g

COOK TIME: 6 hours 10 minutes

DIRECTIONS:

1. Heat 1 tbsp. of oil into a non-stick saucepan on a burner at around medium heat.
2. Cook the turkey cubes with garlic powder, salt, and pepper for around 4-5 minutes.
3. With a frying ladle, move the turkey cubes into the pot of your Crock Pot.
4. Heat the remaining oil into the same saucepan on a burner at around medium heat.
5. Cook the onions for around 4-5 minutes.
6. Place the onion into the pot with the turkey.
7. Put in remaining ingredients except for lemon juice and stir to incorporate.
8. Close the lid of the Crock Pot and set it on the "Low" setting for 6 hours.
9. After cooking time is finished, take off the lid and blend in the lemon juice.
10. Enjoy hot.

Pork & Mushroom Stew

INGREDIENTS:

- Pork loin – 1½ lb. cut into bite-sized pieces
- Fresh mushrooms – 1½ C. sliced
- Medium-sized onions – 2, cut up
- Garlic cloves – 4, cut up
- Chicken broth – 1 C.
- Unsweetened coconut milk – ½ C.
- Paprika – ½ tsp.
- Salt and ground black pepper – as desired

SERVES: 8

PER SERVING:
Calories 342,
Carbs 7.2g,
Fat 14.6g,
Protein 44.1g

COOK TIME: 5 hours

DIRECTIONS:

1. In the pot of your Crock Pot, put pork pieces and the remaining ingredients and stir to incorporate.
2. Close the lid of the Crock Pot and set it on the "Low" setting for 6-8 hours.
3. After cooking time is finished, take off the lid and enjoy hot.

Lamb & Chickpeas Stew

INGREDIENTS:

- Lamb shoulder chops – 2½ lb. cubed
- Dried mint – ½ tsp.
- Ground coriander – 2 tsp.
- Ground cumin – 1 tsp.
- Ground turmeric – ¼ tsp.
- Red chili powder – ¼ tsp.
- Salt and ground black pepper – as desired
- Olive oil – 2 tbsp. divided
- Medium-sized onion – 1, cut up
- Garlic cloves – 4, finely cut up
- Fresh ginger – 1 tbsp. finely cut up
- Chicken broth – 1½ C.

SERVES: 6

PER SERVING:
Calories 675,
Carbs 61.7g,
Fat 24.9g,
Protein 54.9g

- Tomato sauce – 3 C.
- Tomato – ½ C. cut up
- Chickpeas – 1 (15-oz.) can, liquid removed
- Baby potatoes – 2 C. halved
- Fresh spinach – 1 C. cut up

COOK TIME: 6¼ hours

DIRECTIONS:

1. Put lamb cubes, dried mint, and spices into a large-sized bowl and stir thoroughly.
2. Heat 1 tbsp. of oil into a large-sized wok on a burner at around medium heat.
3. Sear the lamb cubes for around 6 minutes.
4. With a frying ladle, move the lamb cubes into the pot of your Crock Pot.
5. Heat the remaining oil into the same wok on a burner at around medium heat.
6. Cook the onion, garlic, and ginger for around 5-6 minutes.
7. Put in broth and tomato sauce and cook until boiling.
8. Place the onion mixture into the Crock Pot with tomatoes, chickpeas, and potatoes and blend to incorporate.
9. Close the lid of the Crock Pot and set it on the "Low" setting for 6 hours.
10. After cooking time is finished, take off the lid and blend in the spinach until wilted.
11. Enjoy hot.

Cod, Tomato & Fennel Stew

INGREDIENTS:

- Large-sized leeks – 2, cut into ¼-inch-thick slices
- Fennel bulb – 1½ lb. cut up
- Tomatoes – 2¼ lb. cut up
- Garlic cloves – 2, cut up
- Fresh parsley sprigs – 8
- Fresh thyme sprigs – 4
- Salt and ground black pepper – as desired
- Dry white wine – ½ C.
- Cod fillets – 2¾ lb.
- Olive oil – 2 tsp.

SERVES: 8

PER SERVING:
Calories 238,
Carbs 14.6g,
Fat 3g,
Protein 38.2g

COOK TIME: 3 hours 40 minutes

DIRECTIONS:

1. In the pot of your Crock Pot, put leeks and remaining ingredients except for cod and oil and stir to incorporate.
2. Close the lid of the Crock Pot and set it on the "High" setting for 3 hours.
3. After cooking time is finished, take off the lid and place the fish on top of the stew.
4. Again, close the lid of the Crock Pot and set it on the "High" setting for 30-40 minutes.
5. After cooking time is finished, take off the lid and discard the herb sprigs.
6. Divide the stew into serving bowls and enjoy with the drizzling of oil.

Chicken & Salsa Chili

INGREDIENTS:

- Boneless chicken breasts – 1 lb.
- Salsa – 2 C.
- Garlic cloves – 2, finely cut up
- Water – 1½ C.
- Ground cumin – 1 tsp.
- Salt and ground black pepper – as desired
- Medium-sized bell peppers – 3, seeded and cut up
- Medium-sized onion – 1, cut up
- Jalapeño pepper – 1, finely cut up
- Red chili powder – 2 tsp.
- Avocado – 1, peeled, pitted, and cut up.

SERVES: 4

PER SERVING:
Calories 201,
Carbs 11.7g,
Fat 9.5g,
Protein 18.7g

COOK TIME: 8 hours

DIRECTIONS:

1. In the pot of your Crock Pot, put chicken, salsa, garlic, water, cumin, salt, and pepper and stir well.
2. Close the lid of the Crock Pot and set it on "Low" setting for 6 hours.
3. Meanwhile, put bell peppers, onion, and jalapeño pepper into a non-stick wok and cook until well roasted.
4. Remove from the burner.
5. After cooking time is finished, take off the lid and place the chicken breasts into a bowl.
6. With 2 forks, shred the chicken.
7. Return the chicken to the Crock Pot with the vegetable mixture, chili powder, avocado, salt, and pepper, and blend thoroughly.
8. Close the lid of the Crock Pot and set it on the "Low" setting for 2 hours.
9. After cooking time is finished, take off the lid and enjoy hot.

Pork & Bacon Chili

INGREDIENTS:

- Medium-sized bell peppers – 2, seeded and cut up
- Medium-sized onion – 1, cut up
- Olive oil – ½ tbsp.
- Lean ground pork – 2 lb.
- Salt and ground black pepper – as desired
- Thick bacon slices – 8, cut up
- Tomatoes – 2 C. cut up
- Ground cumin – 1½ tsp.
- Red chili powder – 2 tsp.
- Cayenne pepper powder – ½ tsp.
- Tomato paste – ¾ C.

SERVES: 6

PER SERVING:
Calories 283,
Carbs 9g,
Fat 17.3g,
Protein 20.4g

COOK TIME: 6 hours 10 minutes

DIRECTIONS:

1. In the pot of your Crock Pot, put the bell peppers and onion.
2. Heat oil in a large-sized wok on a burner at around medium-high heat.
3. Cook pork with salt and pepper for around 4-5 minutes.
4. Shift the pork into the pot with the onion mixture.
5. Put the bacon into the same wok and cook for 4-5 minutes.
6. Place cooked bacon and tomatoes over pork and sprinkle with spices.
7. Pour tomato paste on top.
8. Close the lid of the Crock Pot and set it on the "Low" setting for 6 hours.
9. After cooking time is finished, take off the lid and enjoy hot.

Beef & Zucchini Chili

INGREDIENTS:

- Olive oil – 1 tbsp.
- Lean ground beef – 1 lb.
- Medium-sized onion – 1, cut up
- Medium-sized bell pepper – 1, cut up
- Zucchini – 8 oz. sliced
- Garlic cloves – 2, finely cut up
- Diced tomatoes – 3 C. canned
- Paprika – 2 tbsp.
- Cayenne pepper powder – 1 tbsp.
- Jalapeño pepper – 1, cut up.
- Almond butter – 2 tbsp.
- Salt and ground black pepper – as desired

SERVES: 6

PER SERVING:
Calories 304,
Carbs 9.6g,
Fat 15.6g,
Protein 32g

COOK TIME: 6 hours 10 minutes

DIRECTIONS:

1. Heat oil into a large-sized wok on a burner at around medium heat.
2. Cook the beef for around 4-5 minutes.
3. With a frying ladle, place the beef into the pot of your Crock Pot.
4. Put onion, bell pepper, zucchini, and garlic into the same wok and cook for around 4-5 minutes.
5. Shift the zucchini mixture into the pot with the beef.
6. Put in the remaining ingredients and blend to incorporate.
7. Close the lid of the Crock Pot and set it on the "Low" setting for 8 hours.
8. After cooking time is finished, take off the lid and enjoy hot.

Lentil Chili

INGREDIENTS:

- Red lentils – 2 C. rinsed
- Bell peppers – 2, seeded and cut up
- Carrot – 1, peeled and cut up
- Medium-sized onion – 1, cut up
- Jalapeño pepper – 1, finely cut up
- Garlic cloves – 3, finely cut up
- Diced tomatoes – 1 (28-oz.) can, with the juices
- Tomato paste – 2 tbsp.
- Dried oregano – 1 tsp.
- Red chili powder – 2 tbsp.
- Ground cumin – 2 tsp.
- Smoked paprika – 1 tsp.
- Vegetable broth – 3-4 C.
- Salt and ground black pepper – as desired

SERVES: 6

PER SERVING:
Calories 313,
Carbs 53.5g,
Fat 2.5g,
Protein 21.6g

COOK TIME: 6 hours

DIRECTIONS:

1. In the pot of your Crock Pot, put lentils and the remaining ingredients and stir to incorporate.
2. Close the lid of the Crock Pot and set it on the "Low" setting for 5-6 hours.
3. After cooking time is finished, take off the lid and enjoy hot.

Three Beans Chili

INGREDIENTS:

- Non-stick baking spray
- Onion – 1 C. cut up
- Carrot – 1 C. peeled and cut up
- Bell pepper – 1 C. seeded and cut up
- Celery – 1 C. cut up
- Tomato sauce – 1 (15-oz.) can
- Diced fire-roasted tomatoes – 1 (15-oz.) can
- Red kidney beans – 1 (15-oz.) can, liquid removed
- Black beans – 1 (15-oz.) can, liquid removed
- Pinto beans – 1 (15-oz.) can, liquid removed

- Granulated garlic powder – 1 tsp.
- Ground cumin – 1 tsp.
- Smoked paprika – 1 tsp.
- Red chili powder – 1 tsp.
- Salt – as desired
- Hot sauce – 2 tbsp.
- Lime juice – 1 tbsp.

SERVES: 6

PER SERVING:
Calories 313,
Carbs 59.3g,
Fat 1.7g,
Protein 18.8g

COOK TIME: 7 hours

DIRECTIONS:

1. In the pot of your Crock Pot, put onion and remaining ingredients except for hot sauce and lime juice and blend to incorporate.
2. Close the lid of the Crock Pot and set it on the "Low" setting for 6-7 hours.
3. After cooking time is finished, take off the lid and blend in the hot sauce and lime juice.
4. Enjoy hot.

Notes

....

....

....

....

....

....

....

VEGETARIAN & SIDE DISHES RECIPES

Black-Eyed Peas with Spinach

INGREDIENTS:

- Olive oil – 1 tbsp.
- Large-sized onion – 1, roughly cut up
- Dried black-eyed peas – 1 lb. sorted and rinsed
- Fresh spinach – 2 lb. cut up
- Garlic cloves – 3, cut up
- Chicken broth – 4 C.
- Tomato paste – 3 tbsp.
- Apple cider vinegar – 2 tbsp.
- Bay leaves – 2
- Red pepper flakes – ½ tsp.
- Salt and ground black pepper – as desired

SERVES: 6

PER SERVING:
Calories 164,
Carbs 23.4g,
Fat 5g,
Protein 11g

COOK TIME: 7 hours 5 minutes

DIRECTIONS:

1. Cut thick stems from the spinach and then cut the leaves into ½-inch ribbons crosswise.
2. In a large-sized wok, heat oil on the burner at around medium heat and sauté onion for around 4-5 minutes.
3. Put the onion into the pot of your Crock Pot.
4. Put in peas and remaining ingredients and stir to incorporate.
5. Close the lid of the Crock Pot and set it on the "Low" setting for 6-7 hours.
6. After cooking time is finished, take off the lid and enjoy hot.

Wild Rice & Mushroom Pilaf

INGREDIENTS:

- Wild rice – 1½ C. rinsed
- Sliced mushrooms – 1 (4-oz.) can, with liquid
- Scallion – ¼ C. cut up
- Unsalted butter – 1 tbsp. melted
- Vegetable broth – 2 (14-oz.) cans
- Salt and ground black pepper – as desired
- Dried cranberries – 1/3 C.
- Almonds – ½ C. cut up

SERVES: 6

PER SERVING:
Calories 235,
Carbs 33.7g,
Fat 7.1g,
Protein 10.9g

DIRECTIONS:

COOK TIME: 5¼ hours

1. In the pot of your Crock Pot, stir together the rice and the remaining ingredients except cranberries and almonds.
2. Close the lid of the Crock Pot and set it on the "Low" setting for 4-5 hours.
3. After cooking time is finished, take off the lid and immediately stir in cranberries and almonds.
4. Close the lid of the Crock Pot and set it on the "Low" setting for 15 minutes.
5. After cooking time is finished, take off the lid and enjoy moderately hot.

Chickpeas with Tomatoes

INGREDIENTS:

- Non-stick baking spray
- Unsalted butter – 1 tbsp.
- Medium-sized onions – 2, cut up
- Fresh ginger – 1 tbsp. finely cut up
- Garlic cloves – 2, finely cut up
- Jalapeño peppers – 2, seeded and finely cut up
- Ground cumin – 2 tsp.
- Ground coriander – 1 tsp.
- Paprika – 2 tsp.
- Ground turmeric – 1 tsp.
- Ground cinnamon – 1 tsp.
- Diced tomatoes – 1 (14-oz.) can with liquid
- Chickpeas – 2 (15-oz.) cans, liquid removed and rinsed
- Vegetable broth – 2/3 C.
- Salt and ground black pepper – as desired
- Lemon juice – 2 tbsp.
- Fresh cilantro – 2 tbsp. cut up

SERVES: 6

PER SERVING:
Calories 231,
Carbs 40.8g,
Fat 4.3g,
Protein 9.1g

COOK TIME: 6 hours 10 minutes

DIRECTIONS:

1. Spray the pot of your Crock Pot with baking spray.
2. In a large-sized wok, melt butter on a burner at around medium heat.
3. Cook the onions for around 8-9 minutes, mixing occasionally.
4. Put in ginger, garlic, jalapeño peppers, and spices and sauté for 1 minute more.
5. Put in tomatoes with liquid and blend to incorporate.
6. Put the mixture into the pot of your Crock Pot.
7. Put in remaining ingredients except for lemon juice and cilantro and blend to incorporate.
8. Close the lid of the Crock Pot and set it on the "Low" setting for 6 hours.
9. After cooking time is finished, take off the lid and blend in lemon juice.
10. Enjoy hot with the decoration of cilantro.

Red Kidney Beans Curry

INGREDIENTS:

- Canola oil – 1 tbsp.
- Medium-sized onion – 1, cut up
- Fresh ginger – 1 tbsp. finely cut up
- Garlic – 1 tsp. finely cut up
- Curry powder – 3 tsp.
- Ground cumin – ½ tsp.
- Red pepper flakes – ¼ tsp. crushed
- Tomato paste – 6 oz.
- Plain Greek yogurt – 12 oz.
- Water – ½ C.
- Pinto beans – 3 (15-oz.) cans, liquid removed
- Fresh parsley – ¼ C. cut up

SERVES: 8

PER SERVING:
Calories 303,
Carbs 51.4g,
Fat 3.6g,
Protein 18.1g

COOK TIME: 10 hours

DIRECTIONS:

1. In a large-sized wok, heat oil on a burner at around medium heat.
2. Cook the onion for around 4-5 minutes.
3. Put in the ginger, garlic, curry powder, and spices and sauté for around 1 minute.
4. Blend in tomato paste, yogurt, and water, and immediately take off the burner.
5. In the pot of your Crock Pot, put the beans.
6. Pour the yogurt mixture over the beans and lightly stir to incorporate.
7. Close the lid of the Crock Pot and set it on the "Low" setting for 8-10 hours.
8. After cooking time is finished, take off the lid and enjoy hot with the decoration of parsley.

Lentil Sloppy Joes

INGREDIENTS:

- Green lentils – 1 C. rinsed
- Bell pepper – ½, seeded and cut up
- Onion – 1, cut up
- Diced tomatoes – 1 (15-oz.) can
- Tomato paste – ¼ C.
- Dried parsley – 2 tsp.
- Dried oregano – 1 tsp.
- Garlic powder – 1 tbsp.
- Red chili powder – 1 tbsp.
- Cayenne pepper powder – 1/8 tsp.
- Salt and ground black pepper – as desired
- Lemon juice – 1 tbsp.
- Vegetable broth – 1½ C.
- Whole-wheat burger buns – 8

SERVES: 8

PER SERVING:
Calories 324,
Carbs 58.5g,
Fat 3.4g,
Protein 16.5g

COOK TIME: 8 hours

DIRECTIONS:

1. In the pot of your Crock Pot, put lentils and the remaining ingredients except for buns and stir to incorporate.
2. Close the lid of the Crock Pot and set it on the "Low" setting for 7-8 hours.
3. After cooking time is finished, take off the lid and blend the mixture.
4. Place the lentil mixture in buns and enjoy.

Halloumi & Tomato Curry

INGREDIENTS:

- Cardamom pods – 8
- Cumin seeds – 2 tsp.
- Fenugreek seeds – 1 tsp.
- Ground turmeric – 1 tsp.
- Cayenne pepper powder – ½ tsp.
- Diced tomatoes – 1 (14-oz.) can
- Medium-sized onion – 1, cut up
- Garlic cloves – 2, cut up
- Fresh ginger – 1 (1-inch) piece, grated
- Unsalted butter – 2 tbsp. melted
- Tomato puree – 1 tbsp.
- Mango chutney – 1 tbsp.

SERVES: 4

PER SERVING:
Calories 490,
Carbs 14.8g,
Fat 37.5g,
Protein 26.3g

For the Curry:
- Halloumi cheese – 1 lb. cubed
- Cinnamon stick – 1
- Double cream – ¼ C.
- Fresh cilantro leaves – ¼ C. roughly cut up

COOK TIME: 5¼ hours

DIRECTIONS:

1. For the sauce, remove the seeds from the cardamom pods.
2. With a pestle and mortar, crush the cardamom seeds, cumin, fenugreek, turmeric, and cayenne until ground.
3. Put spice mixture and remaining sauce ingredients into a medium-sized bowl and stir to incorporate.
4. Pour the sauce into the pot of your Crock Pot and stir in the halloumi and cinnamon stick.
5. Close the lid of the Crock Pot and set it on the "Low" setting for 3-5 hours.
6. After cooking time is finished, take off the lid and discard the cinnamon stick.
7. Put in cream and stir to incorporate.
8. Close the lid of the Crock Pot and set it on the "Low" setting for 15 minutes.
9. After cooking time is finished, take off the lid and enjoy hot.

Pumpkin Curry

INGREDIENTS:

- Vegetable oil – 2 tsp.
- Medium-sized onion – 1, sliced
- Garlic cloves – 2, cut up
- Fresh ginger – 1 (2-inch) piece, grated
- Red chiles – 1-2, seeded and sliced
- Tomato paste – 3 tbsp.
- Ground coriander – 2 tsp.
- Ground cumin – 2 tsp.
- Red chili powder – 1 tsp.
- Pumpkin – 2 lb. peel, seeded and cut into 1-inch pieces
- Diced tomatoes – 1 (18-oz.) can
- Full-fat coconut milk – 6 oz.
- Vegetable stock cube – 1, crumbled
- Salt and ground black pepper – as desired
- Fresh cilantro – 3 tbsp. cut up

SERVES: 6

PER SERVING:
Calories 137,
Carbs 8.4g,
Fat 10.9g,
Protein 2.2g

COOK TIME: 6 hours 13 minutes

DIRECTIONS:

1. Heat oil into a medium-sized wok on a burner at around medium heat.
2. Cook the onion with 1/8 tsp. of salt for around 10 minutes, mixing from time to time.
3. Blend in the garlic and chilies and stir-fry for around 2 minutes.
4. Put in tomato paste and spices and stir-fry for around 1 minute.
5. Put the onion mixture into the pot of your Crock Pot.
6. Close the lid of the Crock Pot and set it on the "Low" setting for 6 hours.
7. After cooking time is finished, take off the lid and enjoy hot with the decoration of cilantro.

Mushrooms & Green Beans Casserole

INGREDIENTS:

- French's fried onions – 1 (6-oz.) can, divided
- Fresh green beans – 2 lb. cut into 1-inch pieces
- Refrigerated Alfredo sauce – 1 (10-oz.) container
- Diced water chestnuts – 1 (8-oz.) can, liquid removed
- Mushrooms – 1 (6-oz.) jar, liquid removed and sliced
- Parmesan cheese – 1 C. grated
- Ground black pepper – ½ tsp.

SERVES: 8

PER SERVING:
Calories 402,
Carbs 44.7g,
Fat 18.3g,
Protein 12.6g

COOK TIME: 4 hours

DIRECTIONS:

1. In the pot of your Crock Pot, put half of the fried onions and the remaining ingredients and stir to incorporate.
2. Close the lid of the Crock Pot and set it on the "Low" setting for 4 hours.
3. After cooking time is finished, take off the lid and enjoy hot with the topping of the remaining fried onions.

Broccoli Casserole

INGREDIENTS:

- Non-stick baking spray
- Frozen broccoli – 6 C. cut up and partially thawed
- Onion – ¼ C. cut up
- Condensed cream of celery soup – 1 (10¾-oz.) can, undiluted
- Cheddar cheese – 1½ C. shredded and divided
- Worcestershire sauce – ½ tsp.
- Ground black pepper – ¼ tsp.
- Butter-flavored crackers – 1 C. crushed
- Unsalted butter – 2 tbsp.

SERVES: 10

PER SERVING:
Calories 162,
Carbs 10.1g,
Fat 11g,
Protein 6.7g

COOK TIME: 3 hours 10 minutes

DIRECTIONS:

1. Spray the pot of your Crock Pot with baking spray.
2. Put broccoli, soup, onion, 1 C. of cheese, Worcestershire sauce, and pepper into a large bowl and stir to incorporate.
3. Put the broccoli mixture into the pot of the Crock Pot and sprinkle with crackers.
4. Place the butter on top in the shape of dots.
5. Close the lid of the Crock Pot and set it on the "High" setting for 2½-3 hours.
6. After cooking time is finished, take off the lid and sprinkle with the remaining cheese.
7. Close the lid of the Crock Pot and set it on the "High" setting for 10 minutes.
8. After cooking time is finished, take off the lid and enjoy.

Potato Salad

INGREDIENTS:

- Medium-sized potatoes – 4
- Hard-boiled eggs – 4, peeled and cut up
- Celery – 1 C. cut up
- Onion – ½ C. cut up
- Prepared mustard – 1 tbsp.
- Celery salt – ¼ tsp.
- Garlic salt – ¼ tsp.
- Mayonnaise – ½ C.

SERVES: 4

PER SERVING:
Calories 338,
Carbs 43.3g,
Fat 14.6g,
Protein 9.9g

COOK TIME: 8 hours

DIRECTIONS:

1. Wrap the potatoes into separate pieces of foil and place them into the pot of your Crock Pot.
2. Close the lid of the Crock Pot and set it on the "Low" setting for 6-8 hours.
3. After cooking time is finished, take off the lid and place the potatoes into a bowl.
4. Put them aside to cool.
5. After cooling, chop the potatoes.
6. Put potatoes and remaining ingredients into a large-sized salad dish and gently stir to incorporate.
7. Put the salad dish into your refrigerator to chill before enjoying it.

Braised Kale

INGREDIENTS:

- Olive oil – 1 tbsp.
- Small-sized onion – 1, cut up
- Fresh kale – 1½ lb. tough ribs removed and cut up
- Vegetable broth – 2 C.
- Salt and ground black pepper – as desired

SERVES: 6

PER SERVING:
Calories 69,
Carbs 7g,
Fat 3.3g,
Protein 3.9g

COOK TIME: 4 hours 10 minutes

DIRECTIONS:

1. Heat the oil into a large-sized wok on a burner at around medium heat.
2. Cook the onion for around 5-7 minutes.
3. Put in the kale and cook for 2-3 minutes.
4. Put the kale mixture into the pot of your Crock Pot.
5. Put in the remaining ingredients and blend to incorporate.
6. Close the lid of the Crock Pot and set it on the "Low" setting for 3½-4 hours.
7. After cooking time is finished, take off the lid and enjoy hot

Braised Cabbage & Apple

INGREDIENTS:

- Unsalted butter – 2 tbsp.
- Small-sized onion – 1, thinly sliced
- Balsamic vinegar – 4 tbsp. divided
- Medium-sized apples – 2, peeled, cored and sliced
- Red cabbage – 1 (2½-lb.) head, cored and cut into thin strips
- Ground allspice – ¼ tsp.
- Salt and ground black pepper – as desired
- Water – ¼ C.

SERVES: 6

PER SERVING:
Calories 190,
Carbs 33.7g,
Fat 6.3g,
Protein 4.2g

COOK TIME: 3 hours 8 minutes

DIRECTIONS:

1. Melt butter into a large-sized wok on a burner at around medium heat.
2. Cook onion for around 3 minutes.
3. Stir in 2 tbsp. of vinegar and cook for around 2 minutes.
4. Add in apples and stir-fry for around 2-3 minutes.
5. Put the apple mixture into the pot of your Crock Pot and stir in the remaining vinegar, cabbage, allspice, salt, pepper, and water.
6. Close the lid of the Crock Pot and set it on the "High" setting for 2-3 hours.
7. After cooking time is finished, take off the lid and enjoy hot.

Glazed Sweet Potatoes

INGREDIENTS:

- Sweet potatoes – 3 lb. peeled and sliced
- Applesauce – 1½ C.
- Brown sugar – 2/3 C.
- Unsalted butter – 3 tbsp. melted
- Ground cinnamon – 1 tsp.
- Pecans – ½ C. cut up

SERVES: 8

PER SERVING:
Calories 362,
Carbs 65.8g,
Fat 10.4g,
Protein 3.6g

COOK TIME: 5 hours

DIRECTIONS:

1. In the pot of your Crock Pot, put the sweet potatoes and the remaining ingredients and stir to incorporate.
2. Close the lid of the Crock Pot and set it on the "Low" setting for 4-5 hours.
3. After cooking time is finished, take off the lid and enjoy.

Corn with Tomatoes

INGREDIENTS:

- Fresh corn – 2 C.
- Diced tomatoes – 1 (14½-oz.) can with juice
- Pimentos – 4-oz. liquid removed and sliced
- Water – ¼ C.
- Unsalted butter – 2 tbsp. sliced
- Medium-sized bell pepper – 1, seeded and diced
- Dried cilantro – 1 tsp.
- Garlic salt – 1 tsp.
- Ground black pepper – ¼ tsp.

SERVES: 8

PER SERVING:
Calories 189,
Carbs 31.6g,
Fat 7.1g,
Protein 5.1g

COOK TIME: 3 hours

DIRECTIONS:

1. In the pot of your Crock Pot, put the corn and the remaining ingredients and stir to incorporate.
2. Close the lid of the Crock Pot and set it on the "Low" setting for 2-3 hours.
3. After cooking time is finished, take off the lid and enjoy hot.

Carrot Mash

INGREDIENTS:

- Large-sized carrots – 3, peeled and roughly cut up
- Unsweetened almond milk – 1¼ C.
- Salt and ground black pepper – as desired
- Half-and-half – ¼ C.
- Unsalted butter – 2 tbsp.

SERVES: 6

PER SERVING:
Calories 68,
Carbs 3.9g,
Fat 5.7g,
Protein 0.6g

DIRECTIONS:

COOK TIME: 2½ hours

1. In the pot of your Crock Pot, put carrot, almond milk, salt, and pepper and blend thoroughly.
2. Close the lid of the Crock Pot and set it on the "High" setting for 1 hour.
3. After cooking time is finished, take off the lid and, with a slotted spoon, skim the browning milk on the sides of the pot.
4. Again, close the lid of the Crock Pot and set it on the "High" setting for 1½ hours.
5. After cooking time is finished, take off the lid and, with a slotted spoon, skim the browning milk on the sides of the pot.
6. With an immersion mixer, mash the carrot to form a smooth mixture.
7. Put in half-and-half and butter and blend thoroughly.
8. Enjoy immediately.

Notes

DESSERT RECIPES

Banana Foster

INGREDIENTS:

- Unsalted butter – ½ C.
- Brown sugar – ¼ C.
- Bananas – 6, peeled and cut into 1-inch slices
- Rum – ¼ C.

SERVES: 4

PER SERVING:
Calories 428,
Carbs 49.3g,
Fat 23.6g,
Protein 2.2g

DIRECTIONS:

COOK TIME: 70 minutes

1. Put butter in the pot of your Crock Pot and set it on the "Low" setting for 10 minutes.
2. Put in brown sugar and stir to incorporate thoroughly.
3. Lightly blend in banana slices and rum.
4. Close the lid of the Crock Pot and set it on the "Low" setting for 1 hour.
5. After cooking time is finished, uncover the Crock Pot and enjoy hot.

Coconut Stuffed Apples

INGREDIENTS:

- Unsalted butter – ½ C. melted
- Almond butter – ¼ C.
- Ground cinnamon – 2 tbsp.
- Ground nutmeg – 1 pinch
- Salt – 1 pinch
- Green apples – 4, cored with bottom intact
- Unsweetened coconut – 3-4 tbsp. shredded
- Water – 1 C.

SERVES: 4

PER SERVING:
Calories 352,
Carbs 34.5g,
Fat 25.7g,
Protein 1.4g

DIRECTIONS:

COOK TIME: 3 hours

1. Put butter, almond butter, cinnamon, nutmeg, and salt into a bowl and stir to incorporate.
2. In the pot of your Crock Pot, arrange the apples.
3. Put the water around the apples.
4. With a small-sized spoon, place the butter mixture into each apple.
5. Top each apple with shredded coconut.
6. Close the lid of the Crock Pot and set it on the "Low" setting for 2-3 hours.
7. After cooking time is finished, uncover the Crock Pot and enjoy moderately hot.

Poached Pears

INGREDIENTS:

- Large-sized pears – 4, peeled
- Apple juice – 1 C.
- Cinnamon sticks – 2
- Walnuts – ¼ C. cut up

SERVES: 4

PER SERVING:
Calories 197,
Carbs 39.6g,
Fat 5g,
Protein 2.7g

DIRECTIONS:

COOK TIME: 1 hours 20 minutes

1. Put apple juice into the pot of your Crock Pot.
2. Arrange the pears with cinnamon sticks over juice.
3. Close the lid of the Crock Pot and set it on the "High" setting for 1 hour, changing the side of the pears once halfway through.
4. After cooking time is finished, uncover the Crock Pot, and with tongs, move pears onto plates.
5. Through a fine mesh sieve, strain the juice into a saucepan.
6. Stir in cinnamon sticks and put the saucepan on a burner at around medium-high heat.
7. Cook the juice until boiling.
8. Cook for around 15 minutes.
9. Take off the syrup from the burner and stir in the walnuts.
10. Top each pear with syrup and enjoy.

Caramel Fondue

INGREDIENTS:

- Soft caramels – 25, unwrapped
- Mini marshmallows – 6 tbsp.
- Whole milk – 6 tbsp.

SERVES: 6

PER SERVING:
Calories 175,
Carbs 35g,
Fat 3.7g,
Protein 2.4g

DIRECTIONS:

COOK TIME: 1 hour

1. In the pot of your Crock Pot, put caramels, marshmallows, and milk and stir to incorporate.
2. Close the lid of the Crock Pot and set it on the "High" setting for 1 hour.
3. After cooking time is finished, uncover the Crock Pot and stir the mixture thoroughly.
4. Enjoy moderately hot.

Fruity Compote

INGREDIENTS:

- Sliced peaches – 2 (29-oz.) cans, liquid removed
- Pear halves – 2 (29-oz.) cans, liquid removed and sliced
- Pineapple chunks – 1 (20-oz.) can, liquid removed
- Apricot halves – 1 (15¼-oz.) can, liquid removed and sliced
- Cherry pie filling – 1 (21-oz.) can

SERVES: 18

PER SERVING:
Calories 167,
Carbs 43.2g,
Fat 0.4g,
Protein 1.3g

COOK TIME: 2 hours

DIRECTIONS:

1. In the pot of your Crock Pot, put fruit and pie filling and stir to incorporate.
2. Close the lid of the Crock Pot and set it on the "High" setting for 2 hours.
3. After cooking time is finished, uncover the Crock Pot and stir the mixture thoroughly.
4. Enjoy moderately hot.

Chocolate Pots de Crème

INGREDIENTS:

- Heavy whipping cream – 2 C.
- Bittersweet chocolate – 8-oz. finely cut up
- Instant espresso powder – 1 tbsp.
- Large-sized egg yolks – 4
- White sugar – ¼ C.
- Salt – ¼ tsp.
- Vanilla extract – 1 tbsp.
- Hot water – 3 C.

SERVES: 6

PER SERVING:
Calories 414,
Carbs 32.6g,
Fat 29g,
Protein 5.5g

COOK TIME: 4 hours

DIRECTIONS:

1. Put cream, chocolate, and espresso into a microwave-safe dish.
2. Microwave on the "High" setting for around 4 minutes, blending after every 30 seconds.
3. Put egg yolks, sugar, and salt into a large-sized bowl and whisk to form a foamy mixture.
4. Slowly add in the cream mixture and whisk to incorporate.
5. Stir in vanilla extract.
6. Pour the mixture into 8 – 4-oz. heatproof jars.
7. Cover each jar tightly.
8. In the pot of your Crock Pot, put hot water.
9. Arrange the jars into the pot.
10. Close the lid of the Crock Pot and set it on the "Low" setting for 4 hours.
11. After cooking time is finished, enjoy moderately hot.

Pumpkin Pudding

INGREDIENTS:
- Non-stick baking spray
- Pumpkin puree – 3 C.
- Unsweetened coconut milk – 2 C.
- Unsweetened applesauce – 1/3 C.
- Eggs – 3
- Unsalted butter – 3 tbsp. melted
- Coconut flour – 3 tbsp.
- Pumpkin pie spice – 2 tsp.
- Baking powder – 1 tsp.
- Vanilla extract – 1 tbsp.

SERVES: 8

PER SERVING:
Calories 529,
Carbs 31.7g,
Fat 42.7g,
Protein 10.6g

COOK TIME: 8 hours

DIRECTIONS:
1. Spray the pot of your Crock Pot with baking spray.
2. Put pumpkin puree and remaining ingredients into a mixer and process to form a smooth mixture.
3. Put the mixture into the pot of your Crock Pot.
4. Close the lid of the Crock Pot and set it on the "Low" setting for 6-8 hours.
5. After cooking time is finished, take off the lid and let the pudding cool slightly.
6. Enjoy moderately hot.

Chocolate Cherry Dump Cake

INGREDIENTS:
- Non-stick baking spray
- Cherry pie filling – 2 (21-oz.) cans
- Chocolate cake mix – 1 (15¼-oz.) package
- Salted butter – 1 C. melted

SERVES: 10

PER SERVING:
Calories 468,
Carbs 61.1g,
Fat 24g,
Protein 3.4g

COOK TIME: 3 hours

DIRECTIONS:
1. Spray the pot of your Crock Pot with baking spray.
2. Put the cherry pie filling into the pot and then spread it in an even layer.
3. Put cake mix and butter into a medium-sized bowl and stir until just incorporated.
4. Place the cake mixture on top of the pie filling.
5. Close the lid of the Crock Pot and set it on the "High" setting for 2¾-3 hours.
6. After cooking time is finished, take off the lid and place the pot onto a wire rack to cool for around 10 minutes.
7. Carefully turn the cake onto the platter to cool thoroughly.
8. Cut into serving portions and enjoy.

Caramel Pecan Buns

INGREDIENTS:

- Non-stick baking spray

For the Dough:
- Whole milk – 1/3 C.
- Maple syrup – 4 tbsp.
- Unsalted butter – ½ tbsp. melted
- Vanilla extract – 1 tsp.
- Salt – ¼ tsp.
- Yeast – 2¼ tsp.
- Whole-wheat flour – 1½-2 C.

SERVES: 12

PER SERVING:
Calories 159,
Carbs 25.7g,
Fat 5.3g,
Protein 2.6g

COOK TIME: 2¼ hours

For the Caramel Sauce:
- Maple syrup – 4 tbsp.
- Whole milk – 2 tbsp.
- Unsalted butter – 2 tbsp.
- Pecans – ¼ C. cut up

For the Filling:
- Maple syrup – 3 tbsp.
- Ground cinnamon – 1½ tsp.
- Unsalted butter – ½ tbsp. melted

DIRECTIONS:

1. Lightly spray the pot of your Crock Pot with baking spray.
2. For the dough: in a microwave-safe bowl, put milk, maple syrup, butter and vanilla extract.
3. Microwave on High setting for around 1 minute, mixing after every 20 seconds.
4. Stir in yeast and keep aside for about 10-15 minutes or until frothy.
5. Put in flour, ½ C. at a time, and stir to form a non-stick dough.
6. Place dough onto a floured-dusted counter and knead for a few minutes.
7. Put the dough aside until you need to use it.
8. For the caramel sauce: in a small-sized saucepan, put maple syrup, milk, and butter on a burner at around medium-low heat.
9. Cook until the mixture darkens slightly, mixing frequently.
10. Place caramel sauce into the pot of your Crock Pot and sprinkle with pecans, leaving a ½-inch border around the rim.
11. For filling: in a small bowl, put maple syrup and cinnamon and whisk thoroughly.
12. Place dough onto a floured–dusted counter and roll into a 10x14-inch rectangle.
13. Coat the dough rectangle with melted butter, followed by maple syrup mixture, leaving a ½-inch border on both long edges.
14. Carefully roll dough into a log from one long edge to the other.
15. Cut the log into 12 rolls and immediately place each roll into the caramel sauce in the pot.
16. Close the lid of the Crock Pot and set it on the "Keep Warm" setting for 45 minutes.
17. Now, set it on the "Low" setting for 1¼-1½ hours.

Peach Cobbler

INGREDIENTS:

- Non-stick baking spray

For the Topping:
- Almond flour – 1 C.
- Coconut flour – 1/3 C.
- Baking powder – 1 tsp.
- Salt – 1/8 tsp.
- Eggs – 4
- Unsalted butter – ¼ C. Melted
- Unsweetened applesauce – 2½ tbsp.
- Unsweetened almond milk – 2 tbsp.
- Almond extract – ¼ tsp.

SERVES: 8

PER SERVING:
Calories 155,
Carbs 13.2g,
Fat 10.1g,
Protein 4.8g

COOK TIME: 6 hours

For the Filling:
- Peaches – 6 C. pitted and sliced
- Unsweetened applesauce – 1 tbsp.
- Ground cinnamon – ½ tbsp.
- Ground nutmeg – 1/8 tsp.
- Salt – 1/8 tsp.

DIRECTIONS:

1. Spray the pot of your Crock Pot with baking spray.
2. For the filling, put the peaches and the remaining ingredients into a bowl and stir to incorporate.
3. For the topping, Add the flours, baking powder, and salt into a large-sized bowl and stir to incorporate.
4. Put eggs, butter, applesauce, almond milk, and almond extract into another bowl and whisk to incorporate thoroughly.
5. Put the egg mixture into the flour mixture and stir until just incorporated.
6. In the pot of your Crock Pot, put the filling mixture.
7. Top with the topping mixture.
8. Close the lid of the Crock Pot and set it on the "Low" setting for 4-6 hours.
9. After cooking time is finished, take off the lid and enjoy moderately hot.

Notes

BROTHS & SAUCES RECIPES

Chicken Broth

INGREDIENTS:

- Non-stick baking spray
- Bone-in chicken pieces – 2½ lb.
- Celery stalks – 2, cut up
- Carrots – 2, cut up
- Onion – 1, quartered
- Dried basil – 1 tbsp.
- Water – 6 C.

SERVES: 5

PER SERVING:
Calories 247,
Carbs 6g,
Fat 15g,
Protein 22g

COOK TIME: 10 hours

DIRECTIONS:

1. In the pot of your Crock Pot, place the chicken pieces and remaining ingredients and stir to incorporate.
2. Close the lid of the Crock Pot and set it on the "Low" setting for 8-10 hours.
3. After cooking time is finished, take off the lid and strain the broth.
4. Enjoy immediately.

Vegetable Broth

INGREDIENTS:

- Non-stick baking spray
- Large-sized carrots – 2, peeled and cut into chunks
- Onion – 1, quartered
- Celery stalks – 3, cut up
- Fresh mushrooms – 3, cut up
- Garlic cloves – 3, cut up
- Bay leaf – 1
- Peppercorns – 4-6
- Salt – 1 tbsp.
- Water – 8 C.

SERVES: 8

PER SERVING:
Calories 17,
Carbs 4g,
Fat 1g,
Protein 1g

DIRECTIONS:

COOK TIME: 6 hours

1. In the pot of your Crock Pot, place vegetables and remaining ingredients and stir to incorporate.
2. Close the lid of the Crock Pot and set it on the "High" setting for 4-6 hours.
3. After cooking time is finished, take off the lid and strain the broth.
4. Enjoy immediately.

Applesauce

INGREDIENTS:

- Large-sized apples – 6, peeled, cored, and cut up
- Water – ½ C.
- Cinnamon sticks – 2
- Lemon juice – 1 tbsp.
- Salt – ¼ tsp.

SERVES: 32

PER SERVING:
Calories 22,
Carbs 5.8g,
Fat 0.1g,
Protein 0.1g

COOK TIME: 4 hours

DIRECTIONS:

1. In the pot of your Crock Pot, put the apples and the remaining ingredients and stir to incorporate.
2. Close the lid of the Crock Pot and set it on the "High" setting for 4 hours.
3. After cooking time is finished, take off the lid and discard the cinnamon sticks.
4. With an immersion blender, blend to form a smooth sauce.
5. Let the sauce cool thoroughly before using.

Tomato Sauce

INGREDIENTS:

- Plum tomatoes – 10, peeled, seeded and crushed
- Small-sized onion – ½, cut up
- Garlic – 1 tsp. finely cut up
- Olive oil – ¼ C.
- Dried oregano – 1 tsp.
- Dried basil – 1 tsp.
- Cayenne pepper powder – 1 tsp.
- Ground cinnamon – 1 pinch
- Salt – 1 tsp.
- Ground black pepper – 1 tsp.

SERVES: 10

PER SERVING:
Calories 68,
Carbs 5.5g,
Fat 5.3g,
Protein 1.2g

COOK TIME: 15 hours

DIRECTIONS:

1. In the pot of your Crock Pot, put tomatoes and remaining ingredients and stir to incorporate.
2. Close the lid of the Crock Pot and set it on the "Low" setting for 10-15 hours.
3. After cooking time is finished, take off the lid and, with an immersion blender, blend to form a smooth sauce
4. Let the sauce cool thoroughly before using.

BBQ Sauce

INGREDIENTS:

- Ketchup – 4½ C.
- Water – 2 C.
- Brown sugar – 1¼ C.
- Apple cider vinegar – 1 C.
- Worcestershire sauce – 1 C.
- Onion – ¾ C. finely cut up
- Prepared yellow mustard – ½ C.
- Garlic cloves – 4, finely cut up
- Lemon peel – 4-5 slices
- Liquid smoke – 2 tsp.
- Unsalted butter – 2 tbsp.
- Salt – 2 tbsp.
- Ground black pepper – 2 tbsp.
- Red chili powder – 2 tbsp.
- Cayenne pepper powder – 1 tsp.

SERVES: 70

PER SERVING:
Calories 35,
Carbs 7.7g,
Fat 0.5g,
Protein 0.4g

COOK TIME: 5 hours

DIRECTIONS:

1. In the pot of your Crock Pot, put the ketchup and the remaining ingredients and stir to incorporate.
2. Close the lid of the Crock Pot and set it on the "High" setting for 3 hours.
3. After cooking time is finished, take off the lid and blend the sauce thoroughly.
4. Close the lid of the Crock Pot and set it on the "Low" setting for 2 hours.
5. After cooking time is finished, take off the lid and discard the lemon peel.
6. Let the sauce cool thoroughly before using.

Notes

CONCLUSION

As you close this cookbook, remember it's okay to feel a bit nervous at the start. Cooking is an adventure, and with your crock pot by your side, you're in for a tasty journey. Don't worry if things don't go perfectly the first time – that's all part of the fun! Like any skill, mastering the art of crock pot cooking takes a bit of practice.

So, if your first attempt isn't a gourmet masterpiece, that's perfectly fine. The beauty of the crock pot is its forgiving nature; it turns simple ingredients into something special, even if you're still getting the hang of it. Keep experimenting, tasting, and trying new recipes. With each try, you'll become more confident in the kitchen, and soon enough, you'll be crafting meals that delight your taste buds.

Remember, the joy of cooking lies not just in the final dish but in the process itself. So, embrace the learning curve, savor the moments in the kitchen, and celebrate the small victories. Your crock pot is a patient teacher, and with a sprinkle of patience and a dash of curiosity, you'll soon be creating meals that bring comfort, joy, and a sense of accomplishment.

This page is for your notes

This page is for your notes

Made in the USA
Las Vegas, NV
07 October 2024

96397655R00044